TEXAS TECH

DAILY DEVOTIONS FOR DIE-HARD FANS

RED RAIDERS

Cover design by John Powell and Slynn McMinn
Interior design by Slynn McMinn

Visit us at die-hardfans.com.

Every effort has been made to identify copyright
holders. Any omissions are unintentional. Extra Point
Publishers should be notified in writing immediately
for full acknowledgement in future editions.

Daily Devotions for Die-Hard Fans
Available Titles

ACC
Clemson Tigers
Duke Blue Devils
FSU Seminoles
Georgia Tech Yellow Jackets
North Carolina Tar Heels
NC State Wolfpack
Notre Dame Fighting Irish
Virginia Cavaliers
Virginia Tech Hokies

BIG 10
Michigan Wolverines
Michigan State Spartans
Nebraska Cornhuskers
Ohio State Buckeyes
Penn State Nittany Lions

BIG 12
Baylor Bears
Oklahoma Sooners
Oklahoma State Cowboys
TCU Horned Frogs
Texas Longhorns
Texas Tech Red Raiders
West Virginia Mountaineers

SEC
Alabama Crimson Tide
MORE Alabama Crimson Tide
Arkansas Razorbacks
Auburn Tigers
MORE Auburn Tigers
Florida Gators
Georgia Bulldogs
MORE Georgia Bulldogs
Kentucky Wildcats
LSU Tigers
Mississippi State Bulldogs
Missouri Tigers
Ole Miss Rebels
South Carolina Gamecocks
Tennessee Volunteers
Texas A&M Aggies

and *NASCAR*

Daily Devotions for Die-Hard Kids
Available Titles
Alabama, Auburn, Baylor, Georgia, LSU
Miss. State, Ole Miss, Tennessee, Texas, Texas A&M

---

die-hardfans.com

TEXAS TECH

DAILY
DEVOTIONS
FOR
DIE-HARD
FANS

RED RAIDERS

IN THE BEGINNING

Read Genesis 1, 2:1-3.

"God saw all that he had made, and it was very good" (v. 1:31).

At Texas Tech, the first-ever football game was played before the first-ever session of classes began.

In February 1923, the state legislature approved the establishment of a new college in West Texas. The first faculty meeting was held on Sept. 15, 1925, and Texas Tech formally opened for business with a convocation that afternoon. That same day, the school's first-ever football players gathered for the first time, about two weeks before classes officially began.

That the new "Tech College" would field a football team was never in doubt. Almost as soon as the new school's first president was chosen, the search for a football coach began. From a list of 24 men, Ewing Young "Big Un" Freeland, the line coach at SMU, was named Tech's first athletic director and football coach effective July 1, 1925. His lone assistant coach was Grady Higginbotham, who had played at Texas A&M and, some claimed, at a college in the East after he graduated from A&M.

Enthusiasm for football at Tech showed itself right away in two ways. First, about 120 would-be players showed up for the first practice. Secondly, Freeland's photo in the local paper was blown up to two-column size; the (probably quite disgruntled) new deans and department heads merited only a one-column shot.

Nicknamed the Matadors, that first team consisted mostly of freshmen and sophomores, few of whom had ever played a down of varsity college football. Captain Winfeld "Windy" Nicklaus was a rarity in that he had played a full season of varsity ball at Bucknell as a freshman. A handful of others had played some major-college freshman ball.

Nevertheless, this "Rag Tail Bunch" began the great football tradition at Tech on Oct. 3, 1925, before classes had started, tying the McMurry Indians of McMurry College in Abilene 0-0.

Beginnings are important, but what we make of them is even more important. Consider, for example, how far the Texas Tech football program has come since that first game. Every morning, you get a gift from God: a new beginning. God hands to you as an expression of divine love a new day full of promise and the chance to right the wrongs in your life. You can use the day to pay a debt, start a new relationship, replace a burned-out light bulb, tell your family you love them, chase a dream, solve a nagging problem . . . or not.

God simply provides the gift. How you use it is up to you. People often talk wistfully about starting over or making a new beginning. God gives you the chance with the dawning of every new day. You have the chance today to make things right — and that includes your relationship with God.

They had no tradition on which to build their enthusiasm; the towns- people did not know quite what to expect.
— Tech's first-ever football team, described in The Red Raiders

Every day is not just a dawn; it is a precious chance to start over or begin anew.

A RIPE OLD AGE

Read Psalm 92.

"[The righteous] will still bear fruit in old age, they will stay fresh and green, proclaiming, 'The Lord is upright'" *(vv. 14-15).*

Alex Torres was the old man of his Texas Tech football teams.

Torres first made his presence felt in Lubbock in the spring of 2008. In the weight room, his fellow Red Raiders dubbed him "Air Force" before they even knew his name. They knew he had come from the Air Force Academy and that his approach to practice and weightlifting was definitely that of a soldier. They also knew he was older than they were.

In the summer of 2007, just as his six-week program of basic training was beginning, Torres broke his hand. He was given a year off to heal and to ponder his future at the Academy. A star at wide receiver in high school, Torres missed football. He spent the fall working out and sent some tapes around.

Texas Tech offered him the chance to walk on in the spring of 2008, and he decided to take it. He made ends meet through tuition assistance that came with being honorably discharged from the Air Force and part-time work at the Tech golf course.

Eligible to play in 2009, Torres was 22 years old by then, which meant he was surrounded by fellow wideouts all younger than he. They immediately tagged him the Old Man. Nevertheless, he stayed with it, using his "seniority" to lead the younger guys by example, calling it "the best way to be the glue this football team needs. I've really fallen into that role of setting an example of what we expect around here."

Torres also produced on the field. He was an off-and-on starter for four seasons, making receptions in 43-of-45 games in which he played. In 2011, his junior season, he was All-Big 12 Honorable Mention. The highlight of his Tech career came in 2012 when he caught the game-winning touchdown in the 56-53 triple overtime win over No. 21 TCU.

To view someone like Alex Torres as old by age 22 is extreme even for our youth-obsessed culture. Still, we don't like to admit — even to ourselves — that we're not as young as we used to be.

So we keep plastic surgeons in business, dye our hair, buy cases of those miracle wrinkle-reducing creams, and redouble our efforts in the gym. Sometimes, though, we just have to face up to the truth the mirror tells us: We're getting older every day.

It's really all right, though, because aging and old age are part of the natural cycle of our lives, which was God's idea in the first place. God's conception of the golden years, though, doesn't include unlimited close encounters with a rocking chair and nothing more. God expects us to serve him as we are able all the days of our life. Those who serve God flourish no matter their age because the energizing power of God is in them.

[The younger wideouts] call me Old Man. I take a little longer to warm up than they do.
— *Alex Torres*

Servants of God don't ever retire; they keep working until they get the ultimate promotion.

DAY 3

I TOLD YOU SO

Read Matthew 24:15-31.

"See, I have told you ahead of time" (v. 25).

When Ronald Ross finished up his collegiate basketball career, he truly could say "I told you so" to all those coaches who didn't want him. That included his own coach.

Despite an outstanding resume in high school, Ross found himself unrecruited except by a couple of small junior colleges. Texas Tech assistant Pat Knight tried to place him at other schools where he might earn a scholarship. Nobody was interested.

Tech head coach Bob Knight told Ross he could walk on, but he wouldn't receive a scholarship for at least two years. Despite all the naysayers, Ross believed he was good enough to play in the Big 12, and he wanted to prove it to everyone who didn't believe in him. He accepted Knight's offer in the fall of 2001.

Proving himself all the way, Ross became a starter as a sophomore. Just as Knight had said, he received a scholarship before his junior season. He averaged 10.1 points per game in 2003-04, third on the team.

Ross really came into his own his senior year. A team captain, he led the Red Raiders in scoring (17.5 ppg) and steals and was second in rebounding. He was named first team All-Big 12. Oklahoma's head coach said Ross was the best player in the league without the ball because of his ability to get open.

With Ross leading the way, the Red Raiders had a spectacular season in 2004-05, winning 22 games and advancing to the NCAA Tournament's Sweet Sixteen.

Against third-seeded Gonzaga in the second round, Ross put together an "all-court masterpiece" with 24 points, nine rebounds, four assists, and three steals. He hit the game-winning shot, a three-pointer, with 1:10 left in the 71-69 upset.

Bob Knight said of Ross, "I have never had a player I've had more admiration for." Ross could simply say, "I told you so."

Don't you just hate it in when somebody says, "I told you so"? That means the other person was right and you were wrong; that other person has spoken the truth. You could have listened to that know-it-all in the first place, but then you would have lost the chance yourself to crow, "I told you so."

In our pluralistic age and society, many view truth as relative, meaning absolute truth does not exist. All belief systems have equal value and merit. But this is a ghastly, dangerous fallacy because it ignores the truth that God proclaimed in the presence and words of Jesus.

In speaking the truth, Jesus told everybody exactly what he was going to do: come back and take his faithful followers with him. Those who don't listen or who don't believe will be left behind with those four awful words, "I told you so," ringing in their ears and wringing their souls.

A lot of people doubted me. Having the opportunity to prove people wrong is a good thing.
— *Ronald Ross*

**Jesus matter-of-factly told us what he has planned:
He will return to gather all the faithful to himself.**

DAY 4

ANIMAL KINGDOM

Read Psalm 139:1-18.

"For you created my inmost being; you knit me together in my mother's womb. I praise you because I am fearfully and wonderfully made" (vv. 13-14).

As "a cowboy who just happened to play football," it was only natural that E.J. Holub should ride his horse right on into a Dallas sports bar.

Holub was a two-time All-American center (in 1959 and '60) who as a senior in 1960 became the first Red Raider to be named All-Southwest Conference. He was the first player in Texas Tech football history to have his jersey number retired (55) and the first Red Raider to be inducted into the College Football Hall of Fame (1986). He was inducted into the Texas Tech Athletic Hall of Honor in 1977. He is the only player in history to start one Super Bowl on offense and another on defense. Holub died in 2019.

Asked once how long he had been interested in football, Holub famously replied, "Forever." He shared that love of the game, however, with an abiding interest in the Western life of the cowboy and his horse, appropriately named Cowboy.

Holub expressed that interest by dressing as a cowboy, "and it wasn't customary back then." When he entered Mike Ditka's Dallas establishment wearing his typical garb, he was usually asked where his horse was. Finally, Holub one day loaded Cowboy into a trailer, drove to Ditka's place, and then unloaded him. He asked someone to hold the doors open "because he was coming in."

Holub and Cowboy ventured into "a really nice place. Not the kind of place you expect to see a mounted horse," said a friend of Holub's, Bobo Echols. Once he got inside, Holub dismounted, kept the reins in his hand, and walked to the bar. Echols said the athletes and sports-type people there barely paid any attention, and Holub acted like "I'm on my horse where I belong."

As an aside, the place "began making money hand over fist when local customers heard of the horse coming in for a visit."

Animals such as Cowboy and Texas Tech's Fearless Champion (named in April 2013) elicit our awe and our respect. Nothing enlivens a trip more than glimpsing turkeys, bears, or deer in the wild. Admit it: You go along with the kids' trip to the zoo because you think it's a cool place too. All that variety of life is mind-boggling. Who could conceive of a horse, a walrus, a moose, or a prairie dog? Who could possibly have that rich an imagination?

But the next time you're in a crowd, look around at the parade of faces. Who could come up with the idea for all those different people? For that matter, who could conceive of you? You are unique, a masterpiece who will never be duplicated.

The master creator, God Almighty, is behind it all. He thought of you and then brought you into being. If you had a manufacturer's label, it might say, "Lovingly, fearfully, and wonderfully handmade in Heaven by #1 — God."

[Mike] Ditka kept riding me, so I just took my horse and went in there.
— E.J. Holub on riding Cowboy into Ditka's Dallas sports bar

**You may consider some painting or an animal
a work of art, but the real masterpiece is you.**

DAY 5

HOMEBODIES

Read 2 Corinthians 5:1-10.

"We . . . would prefer to be away from the body and at home with the Lord" (v. 8).

On Dec. 12, 2012, Kliff Kingsbury came home.

On that day, Texas Tech director of athletics Kirby Hocutt announced that Kingsbury had been hired as the fifteenth head football coach in Red Raider history. At 33, Kingsbury overnight became the youngest head football coach in a major conference.

The hiring completed a meteoric rise for Kingsbury. He took over at his alma mater only five years after beginning his coaching career at Houston. "I thought I would still be playing right now, to be honest," he admitted. "I couldn't have dreamt of it." In a video posted on Twitter that announced the hiring, Kingsbury said the last few days had been a whirlwind, "but I couldn't be happier — beyond ecstatic to be back."

And he *was* back, back at the school from which he graduated in 2001. Tech runs deeper than that for Kingsbury, however. He was the first in a line of Tech quarterbacks developed under the tutelage of head coach Mike Leach. From 1999-2002, he completed more than 1,000 passes and threw for more than 12,000 yards. He set 39 school records, sixteen Big 12 marks, and seventeen NCAA standards.

The more traditional announcement of the new coach's hiring was made at a hastily arranged press conference only two hours after the video appeared. "I loved it out here," the native of New Braunfels said. "I'm thrilled to be back." From the exuberant reception Kingsbury received at his homecoming, Hocutt had clearly hit a home run with Raider fans. "I think it's a great day for Texas Tech," declared Tech Chancellor Kent Hance.

Kingsbury coached at the place that was home to him through the 2018 football season. In January 2019, he was hired as the head coach of the NFL's Arizona Cardinals.

Home is not necessarily a matter of geography. It may be that place you share with your spouse and your children, whether it's West Texas or Alaska. You may feel at home when you return to Lubbock, as Kliff Kingsbury did, and wonder why you were eager to leave in the first place. Maybe the home you grew up in still feels like an old shoe, a little worn but comfortable and inviting.

It is no mere happenstance that among the circumstances of life that we most abhor is that of being homeless. That dread results from the sense of home God planted in us. Our God is a God of place, and our place is with him.

Thus, we may live a few blocks away from our parents and grandparents or we may relocate every few years, but we will still sometimes feel as though we don't really belong no matter where we are. We don't; our true home is with God in the place Jesus has gone ahead to prepare for us. We are homebodies and we are perpetually homesick.

Let me tell you. It's good to be home.
— Kliff Kingsbury on returning to Texas Tech

We are continually homesick for our real home,
which is with God in Heaven.

DAY 6

HOW DISAPPOINTING!

Read Ezra 3.

*"Many of the older priests and Levites and family heads,
who had seen the former temple, wept aloud when they
saw the foundation of this temple being laid, while many
others shouted for joy" (v. 12).*

Everyone associated with Texas Tech football was once disappointed that a player was named All-America.

With World War II claiming many of college football's best players, Tech's prospects in 1944 took a turn for the better when fullback Walt Schlinkman showed up for practice. He had broken his leg in a scrimmage before the 1943 season began, and head coach Dell Morgan had not counted on him for 1944.

Schlinkman scored a touchdown in his first game back and was off and running on a stellar career. The *Lubbock Avalanche-Journal* soon touted him as a "worthy candidate for All-American honors." In the 20-0 win over New Mexico, Schlinkman passed for the first TD, rushed for the second, kicked the extra point, played a sterling defensive game, punted, and rushed for 123 yards.

He disappointed no one in his senior season of 1945, though he battled a shoulder injury for much of the year. Against West Texas State Teachers College, for instance, because of the injury he didn't come into the game until the third quarter. He promptly intercepted a pass and took it 34 yards for a touchdown. He went 30 yards for the second score in the fourth quarter in the 12-6 win.

At season's end, Schlinkman, guard Floyd Lawhorn, and end R.W. Moyes were named to UPI's Little All-America team. The latter two were delighted with the recognition, but Morgan, the players, the administration, and the student body were disappointed with Schlinkman's inclusion. They felt he deserved more than being named among the best players from the schools that didn't play a major schedule.

We know disappointment. Our dreams shatter; friends betray us; we lose our jobs through no fault of our own; emotional distance grows between us and our children; the Red Raiders lose.

Disappointment occurs when something or somebody fails to meet the expectations we have for them. Since people are people and can't do anything about that, they inevitably will disappoint us. What is absolutely crucial to our day-to-day living, therefore, is not avoiding disappointment but handling it.

One approach is to act as the old people of Israel did at the dedication of the temple. Instead of joyously celebrating the construction of a new place of worship, they wailed and moaned about the lost glories of the old one. They chose disappointment over lost glories rather than the wonders of the present reality.

Disappointment can paralyze us all, but only if we lose sight of an immutable truth: Our lives may not always be what we wish they were, but God is still good to us.

There's nothing disappointing about that.

I am disappointed about Schlinkman.
— Dell Morgan on Walt Schlinkman's being named Little All-America

Even in disappointing times, we can be confident that God is with us and therefore life is good.

CELEBRATION TIME

Read Luke 15:1-10.

"There is rejoicing in the presence of the angels of God over one sinner who repents" (v. 10).

The bewildered reporter was alone on the Texas Tech campus. Then the game ended — and the celebration began.

On April 4, 1993, a reporter from Atlanta arrived on campus to cover the reaction if the Tech women's basketball team won the national championship. To his dismay, there was no one around. So he parked his car near Memorial Circle, sat on the hood, and listened to the final seconds of the game on the radio all by his lonesome. "It was so quiet, he could hear the birds chirping," said Marsha Sharp, the team's coach.

But when the game ended with a Tech win over Ohio State, the reporter found himself in the midst of complete chaos. Students poured out of the dorms onto Memorial Circle. They danced, whooped it up, and swam in the fountains. People took to their cars to ride around, blow their horns, and just generally make a bunch of racket and create a monstrous traffic jam.

Senior guard Krista Kirkland (Gerlich) always regretted not being on campus for the immediate, spontaneous celebration of the national championship. "We celebrated together in our own way (in Atlanta)," she said, "but we also wanted to be back on campus to celebrate with the students."

When the players stepped off the plane in Lubbock the next

night, they found themselves virtually alone like that reporter. "I remember wondering where everyone was," said forward Sheryl Swoopes. When the players climbed into limousines, she said, "We thought we were going . . . to get in our cars and go home."

Not so. When the limos hit University Avenue, Swoopes and her teammates saw why no one was at the airport. Wild and crazy Tech fans lined the streets with banners to cheer the champs. About 40,000 more fans welcomed them home at Jones Stadium. All in all, it was the biggest celebration Texas Tech has ever had.

Tech won again. You got that new job or that promotion. You just held your newborn child in your arms. Life has those grand moments that call for celebration. You may jump up and down and scream in a wild frenzy at Jones Stadium or share a quiet, sedate candlelight dinner at home — but you celebrate.

Consider then a celebration that is beyond our imagining, that fills every corner of the very home of God and the angels. Imagine a celebration in Heaven, which also has its grand moments.

Those grand moments are touched off when someone comes to faith in Jesus. Heaven itself rings with the joyous sounds of the singing and dancing of the celebrating angels. Even God rejoices when just one person — you or someone you have introduced to Christ? — turns to him. When you said "yes" to Christ, you made the angels dance. Most importantly of all, you made God smile.

We basically missed the best party ever on campus.
— Krista Kirkland Gerlich on being in Atlanta after winning the title

God himself joins the angels in heavenly celebration when even a single person turns to him through faith in Jesus.

DAY 8

IN A WORD

Read Matthew 12:33-37.

"For out of the overflow of the heart the mouth speaks. The good man brings good things out of the good stored up in him, and the evil man brings evil things out of the evil stored up in him" (vv. 34b-35).

With time running out and the Red Raiders down by three, Graham Harrell expected to hear some typically motivational words from head coach Mike Leach. Instead, he got simple, deadpan instructions. They worked.

Harrell is a Tech legend. As the Raiders' starting quarterback from 2006-08, he set an NCAA record with 134 passing touchdowns and became the first player in NCAA history to post multiple 5,000-yard passing seasons.

On Sept. 30, 2006, the 3-1 Red Raiders trailed the 4-0 Aggies of Texas A&M 27-24 with only 2:12 left in the game at Kyle Field. A&M had just scored the go-ahead touchdown, and Harrell and his offensive mates were staring at 80 yards of grass they had to navigate after the kickoff.

The sophomore quarterback stood next to Leach ready to enter the game, delaying a moment to hear his coach's usual motivational declarations after he called the first play. Instead, Leach issued what amounted to a simple, direct order to his quarterback: go score a touchdown.

Harrell moved the team to the Aggie 37 with less than a minute to play. When A&M blitzed, Harrell was ready. So was running back Shannon Woods, who kept an onrushing A&M defender off Harrell long enough for him to fling the ball downfield to senior wide receiver Robert Johnson. He outfought an Aggie defender for the game-winning catch and the 31-27 win.

As Harrell put it, the crowd went from "absolutely crazy to absolutely silent." They had nothing to say; the Raiders had said it all in carrying out their coach's pithy instructions.

These days, everybody's got something to say and likely as not a place to say it. Talk has really become cheap as the 24-hour media scramble to fill their programming with just about anyone who is willing to expound on just about anything.

But words still have power, and that includes not just those of the talking heads, hucksters, and pundits on television, but ours also. Our words are perhaps the most powerful force we possess for good or for bad. The words we speak today can belittle, wound, humiliate, and destroy. They can also inspire, heal, protect, and create. Our words both shape and define us. They also reveal to the world the depth of our faith.

We should never make the mistake of underestimating the power of the spoken word. After all, speaking the Word was the only means Jesus had to get his message across — and look what he managed to do.

We must always watch what we say because others sure will.

He would tell me the first play and usually say something motivational.
— Graham Harrell on head coach Mike Leach

Choose your words carefully; they are the most powerful force you have for good or for bad.

DAY 9

THE RIGHT MAN

Read Exodus 3:1-12.

"So now, go. I am sending you to Pharaoh to bring my people the Israelites out of Egypt" (v. 10).

The first time Spike Dykes applied to head up the Tech football program, he wasn't the right man for the job. The second time — well, it took him about an hour to get hired.

Dykes came to Lubbock in 1984 as an assistant to Jerry Moore. Given the peripatetic nature of his coaching career — Tech was his twelfth stop in 25 years — Dykes said it took a couple of years for his wife and him to feel safe enough to unpack.

When the head coaching job came open after the 1985 season, Dykes applied. "I didn't think I really had a chance," he said, "but if you're a coordinator, you're supposed to do that." He was right about his chances; David McWilliams got the job.

Dykes assumed he had been wise not to unpack because he expected McWilliams to do what new coaches invariably did: bring in their own people. The two were friends from the days when they coached against each other in high school, though, and McWilliams kept Dykes on as his defensive coordinator.

The 1986 team went 7-4, 5-3 in the Southwest Conference, good enough for Texas to hire McWilliams away. In a rare gesture, Mc-Williams told all ten of his assistants, including Dykes, that they were welcome to join him in Austin. Athletic director T Jones had already stepped up, though. About an hour after McWilliams resigned, Jones offered Dykes the head coaching job. There was no national search and no series of job interviews. Jones knew that Dykes was the right man for the job.

He was. The coach who took a while to unpack wound up as the longest tenured coach in Rec Raider history. His 82 wins is topped only Mike Leach's 84 victories. Dykes coached the team in seven bowl games, and was coach of the year three times in the Southwest Conference and once in the Big 12.

What do you want to be when you grow up? Somehow you are supposed to know the answer to that question when you're a teenager, the time in life when common sense and logic are at their lowest ebb. Long after those halcyon teen years are left behind, you may make frequent career changes. You chase the job that gives you not just financial rewards but also some personal satisfaction and sense of accomplishment.

God, too, wants you in the right job, one that he has designed specifically for you. Though Moses protested that he wasn't the right man, he was indeed God's anointed one, the right man to do exactly what God needed done.

There's a little Moses in all of us. Like him, we shrink before the tasks God calls us to. Like him also, we have God-given abilities, talents, and passions. The right man or woman for any job is the one who works and achieves not for self but for the glory of God.

There was no doubt in my mind that's what we needed.
— Tech AD T Jones on hiring Spike Dykes

Working for God's glory and not your own
makes you the right person for the job,
no matter what it may be.

THE BIG TIME

Read Revelation 21:22-27; 22:1-6.

"They will see his face, and his name will be on their foreheads. . . . And they will reign for ever and ever" (vv. 22:4, 5c).

On May 22, 1956, after years of working and dreaming, Texas Tech hit the big time.

On that day, after being refused in 1927, 1929, 1931, and 1952, Tech was admitted into the Southwest Conference, which had not let a new family into the neighborhood since 1922. The most important single development in the history of Tech athletics to that moment "caused the biggest celebration in Lubbock since the end of World War II."

Tech's admission into the prestigious conference was called "a personal triumph" for DeWitt Weaver, Tech's head football coach and athletic director. That triumph did not come easily, though.

In 1952, Tech officials thought the school would be voted in at the conference meeting, but it didn't happen. "That was one of the darkest days of my stay at Tech," Weaver later said.

As the vote in May of 1956 neared, Athletic Council Chairman Dr. J. William Davis found himself in an awkward position. The Border Conference, of which Tech was a member, was meeting at the same time as the SWC, and Davis was to be installed as the conference president. He explained his predicament, and "they understood and were very good about it."

Anxiety grew as the vote neared. Last-minute calls led Davis to tell Weaver, "We've got it made, Coach." Still, AP Texas sports chief Harold Ratliff, a staunch supporter of Tech's getting into the conference, told Davis, "I think something has gone wrong, Bill. I've heard we aren't going to get in." Davis made another phone call, and his contact told him to get a good night's sleep.

Tech was in. The dream of the big time had come true.

Like Texas Tech, we often look around at our current situation and dream of something bigger. We might look longingly at that vice-president's office or day dream about the day when we're the boss, maybe even of our own business. We may scheme about ways to make a lot of money, or at least more than we're making now. We may even consciously seek out fame and power.

Making it big is just part of the American dream. It's the heart of that which drives immigrants to leave everything they know and come to this country.

The truth is, though, that all of this "big-time" stuff we dream about and so earnestly cherish is small potatoes. If we want to speak of what is the real big-time, we better think about God and his dwelling place in Heaven. There we not only see God and Jesus face to face, but we reign. God puts us in charge.

It just doesn't get any bigger than that — and it's ours for the taking. Or at least for the believing.

It had started with a wish in the '20s, grew to a desire in the '30s, hibernated in the '40s, . . . and rose up on its hind legs in the '50s.
— from The Red Raiders *on Tech's entering the SWC*

Living with God, seeing Jesus, and reigning
in Heaven — now that's big time.

DAY 11

THE REVOLUTIONARY

Read Matthew 3:1-12.

"After me will come one who is more powerful than I, . .
. . He will baptize you with the Holy Spirit and with fire"
(v. 11b).

In just a few years, [Chris] Beard has taken a largely irrelevant Texas Tech [men's basketball] program and turned it into a powerhouse." That is, the veteran coach has pulled off a revolution.

Before Beard was hired in 2016, the Red Raiders had had losing records in five of the six previous seasons. In his second year on the job, Beard had Tech in the NCAA Tournament's Elite Eight. In 2018-19, he led them to the tournament's championship game.

How has he done it? Tech's success has come primarily on the backs of its defense. In 2018-19, they had "the best defense in college basketball . . . but leaving it at that undersells the team's accomplishments."

The thing is, the "Red Raiders' defensive style seems like it shouldn't succeed in an era when the 3-point shot is king." As *The Ringer's* Rodger Sherman wrote, Tech's defense is somewhat out of place in today's game. The primary goal is to defend the middle of the floor, not the 3-point arc. The middle. The problem is that makes it easy for opponents to drive to the baseline.

Which is exactly what the Red Raiders want. When an opponent takes what he has been given, "a wall of Red Raiders help defense will come crashing down on him." Beard's revolution is that he has "forged a group of players who want to get defensive stops more than anything in the world." They went to the "doorstep of a stunning national title because of it."

And when a program plays the best defense in all of men's college basketball, chances are it's not going away.

Throughout recorded history, revolutions on a much grander scale than what has taken place on Texas Tech's basketball court have changed the world. From France to Russia to America to Cuba, revolutions have swept across the world stage, demolishing the past in the process. Even the Industrial Revolution was cataclysmic.

No revolution, however, has ever had an impact on history to match the one wrought by an itinerant preacher some two millennia ago. As God's prophet, John the Baptist saw it coming and preached it. This revolution was different in that what it sought was an end to rebellion. John's call was for repentance, a revolution of the soul, a change that would lead to living the way God has prescribed rather than rebelling against God's word.

This revolution shattered everything about human history in that for the first time God himself became a part of that history. The kingdom of heaven came to Earth in the person of Jesus Christ, a revolutionary such as the world had never seen before and will never see again.

The basketball team has instituted a revolutionary defensive scheme.
– The Ringer's Rodger Sherman, explaining Tech's basketball revolution

All man-made revolutions pale beside the one God wrought when he brought the kingdom of heaven to Earth in Jesus.

UNCERTAIN TIMES

Read Psalm 18:1-6, 20-29.

"The Lord is my rock . . . in whom I take refuge. He is my shield, and the horn of my salvation, my stronghold" (v. 2).

Entering Tech's game against West Virginia, uncertainty surrounded the defense, which was quite strange since it was statistically the best pass defense in the country.

The Red Raiders vs. the Mountaineers on Oct. 13, 2012, was one of the most intriguing matchups of the college football season. Besides being the first-ever Big-12 encounter between the two, the game featured Tech's top-ranked pass defense against WVU's second-ranked passing offense. The oddsmakers were skeptical of Tech's defense despite its lofty ranking and gave WVU the edge.

They had good reason to do so. The Mountaineers waltzed into Jones Stadium undefeated and ranked fifth in the nation with an offense averaging 52 points a game behind quarterback Geno Smith. In their last two games, they had hung 48 points on Texas and 70 on Baylor.

So the Tech defense went out and put on one of the most dominating performances in Red Raider history, though the numbers may not show it. In fact, after the game, the defense fell from first to fourth place in passing defense. They gladly took it after what they did to West Virginia.

The Raiders destroyed WVU 49-14, holding Smith to 275 yards

through the air. "I think we schemed them up perfect and really locked down the run and locked down their big receivers," said senior safety Cody Davis in explaining Tech's success. He had a career-high 13 tackles.

The key to the game was the defense's ability to put pressure on Smith throughout the game. Defensive tackle Kerry Hyder led the rush, teaming with end Dartwan Bush to collapse the pocket several times and send Smith scrambling or throwing in a hurry.

When it was all said and done, one thing was certain: Texas Tech and its defense had dominated the Mountaineers.

Even when we believe Texas Tech will field another great football team, we are uncertain. That's because nothing in sport is a sure thing. If it were, it wouldn't be any fun.

Life is like that. We never know what's in store for us or what's going to happen next. We can be riding high one day with a job promotion, good health, a nice family, and sunny weather. Only a short time later, we can be unemployed, sick, divorced, and/or broke. When we place our trust in life itself and its rewards, we are certain to face uncertain times.

We must search out a haven, a place where we know we can find certainty to ease our trepidation and anxiety about life's uncertainties. We can find that haven, that rock, by dropping to our knees. There, we can find that certainty — every time.

Our life and times are uncertain. The Lord God Almighty is sure — and is only a prayer away.

We kind of fell off last week and kind of took it personal.
— Safety Cody Davis on the disrespected Tech defense

Only God offers certainty amid life's uncertainty.

DAY 13

THE FAME GAME

Read 1 Kings 10:1-10, 18-29.

*"King Solomon was greater in riches and wisdom than
all the other kings of the earth. The whole world sought
audience with Solomon" (vv. 23-24).*

The pressures of the fame generated by being an All-American
at Tech should have been no problem for Denton Fox. After all, he
had already been in a big-time movie.

Fox was the sixth Texas Tech football player to be named first-
team All-America when he received the honor as a senior cornerback in 1969. Head coach JT King didn't recruit him for defense,
though, but as a running back after he averaged more than eight
yards a carry his senior season of high school.

Early on, however, the coaches decided to take advantage of
Fox's size and speed on defense. He was 6-foot-3 and weighed
200 lbs. in a day before the outsized cornerbacks of today's game.
Teammate John David Howard, a safety, said that Fox "was the
fastest guy on the team." He was also "an extremely hard hitter.
Very good on one-on-one coverage."

With all that talent, speed, and size, Fox flourished on defense.
"He had a way of being in the right place at the right time," King
said of his star. "Denton was one of those youngsters who showed
up when you needed him."

After the 1969 season, as was usual then, Fox appeared on the
Bob Hope Christmas Special with his fellow All-Americas. The acco-

lades and the TV appearance weren't his first brush with fame, however. Much of the 1963 movie *Hud*, starring Paul Newman and Patricia Neal, was filmed in and around Claude, Fox's hometown. He and his childhood sweetheart, Sara, who married in 1966, appeared briefly as teenaged extras in the film.

Have you ever wanted to be famous? Hanging out with other rich and famous people, having folks with microphones listen to what you say, throwing money around like toilet paper, meeting adoring and clamoring fans, signing autographs, and posing for the paparazzi before you climb into your imported sports car?

Many of us yearn to be famous, well-known in the places and by the people that we believe matter. That's all fame amounts to: strangers knowing your name and your face.

The truth is that you are already famous where it really does matter, which excludes TV's talking heads, screaming teenagers, rapt moviegoers, or D.C. power brokers. You are famous because Almighty God knows your name, your face, and everything else there is to know about you.

If a persistent photographer snapped you pondering this fame — the only kind that has eternal significance — would the picture show the world unbridled joy or the shell-shocked expression of a mug shot?

[Denton] and [his wife] Sara were in the scene where . . . some kids' dates were walking into the movie. He and Sara were two of those.
— *Tech safety John David Howard on Fox's appearance in* Hud

You're already famous because God
knows your name and your face,
which may be either reassuring or terrifying.

DAY 14

EXCUSES, EXCUSES

Read Luke 9:57-62.

"Another said, 'I will follow you, Lord; but first let me go back and say good-by to my family'" (v. 61).

Under the circumstances, Billy Joe Tolliver's rather bizarre excuse for missing bed check was quite reasonable: Not only did he not know what time it was, he wasn't too sure what *day* it was.

In the spring of 1984, Tolliver flew into Lubbock on a recruiting trip. He was from tiny Boyd (pop. 889) and wasn't at all sure about Texas Tech. One ride into campus changed all that. Tech legend Donny Anderson met him at the airport and accompanied him on the ride to the football offices. "I still remember that ride to campus," Tolliver said years later. "Donny would wave at folks and everyone would wave back. . . . It was just like home. I knew that was where I wanted to be."

After a redshirt season, Tolliver claimed the quarterback spot for four seasons (1985-88). Along the way to an All-SWC career, he crushed virtually every school passing record at the time.

Tolliver's finest performance came in his final game against Oklahoma State in — of all places — Tokyo. He completed 28-of-41 passes for a career-high 446 yards and two touchdowns. The trip didn't come off without a hitch, though.

One night at bed check, Tolliver was nowhere to be found, and the coaches were none too happy about it, visions of carousing dancing in their heads. A manhunt ensued and the truant was discovered on the far side of midnight. He was happily driving golf balls into the night sky at a driving range built on top of a parking garage because of the limited space in the crowded city.

Considering the severe time change involved in the trip from Lubbock to Tokyo, the coaches understood Tolliver's excuse that he didn't have any idea what time it was, accepted his apology, and cut him some slack. As head coach Spike Dykes put it, "We all had some troubles figuring out what time it was. . . . Hey, he was out there getting exercise."

Has some of your most creative thinking involved excuses for not going in to work? Have you discovered that an unintended benefit of computers is that you can always blame them for the destruction of all your hard work? Don't you manage to stammer or stutter some justification when a state trooper pulls you over? We're usually pretty good at making excuses to cover our failures or to get out of something we don't particularly want to do.

That holds true for our faith life also. The Bible is too hard to understand so I won't read it; the weather's too pretty to be shut up in church; praying in public is embarrassing and I'm not very good at it anyway. The plain truth is, though, that whatever excuses we make for not following Jesus wholeheartedly are not good enough.

Jesus made no excuses to avoid dying for us; we should offer none to avoid living for him.

Heck, we weren't sure what DAY it was.
— Spike Dykes on Billy Joe Tolliver's excuse for missing bed check

Try though we might, no excuses can justify
our failure to follow Jesus wholeheartedly.

DAY 15

PAIN RELIEF

Read 2 Corinthians 1:3-7.

"Just as the sufferings of Christ flow over into our lives, so also through Christ our comfort overflows" (v. 5).

For much of the 2007 season, Tech head coach Mike Leach had to practice what he preached: playing with pain.

Leach drew some raised eyebrows when he showed up for the 42-17 win over Iowa State on Oct. 6, 2007, with an elastic sleeve on his right elbow. The subject of the head coach's injury was then broached at his Monday news conference. Leach's first response was, "We don't talk about injuries here at Texas Tech."

The immediate suspect was Leach's leisure-time preoccupation with in-line skating. Just after he moved to Lubbock to begin his work as the football program's strength coach, Bennie Wylie spotted a "sloppily dressed middle-aged man in-line skating down the center of the road" with "cars whizzing past at 30 m.p.h. in both directions." "That lunatic looks a little like Coach," Wylie thought. Then when he pulled alongside the skater, Wylie realized that this lunatic was indeed his new boss.

Leach later explained that he had "calculated that the middle of that particular road was Lubbock's flattest, smoothest surface." For the ever-logical Leach, the busy thoroughfare was thus the most obvious place to start his new hobby no matter how much traffic sped by, each vehicle a serious threat.

But the injury wasn't due to in-line skating. "I've never gotten injured bad on Rollerblades," Leach told the journalists. This particular injury, he explained, came about as a result of an adventure involving his bicycle. He had a flat tire and "tried to fill it and make a run for it, hoping that I could get in before it ran out of air again." He didn't make it. Instead, he went into a slide when he tried a routine turn.

The broken arm was one result of the accident. Leach also suffered abrasions on his right hip and right shoulder and skinned the palms of both hands. Like any athlete, though, he soldiered right on, not letting the pain slow him down.

Since you live on Earth and not in Heaven, you are forced to play with pain. Whether it's a car wreck that left you shattered, the end of a relationship that left you battered, or a loved one's death that left you tattered — pain finds you and challenges you to keep going.

While God's word teaches that you will reap what you sow, life also teaches that pain and hardship are not necessarily the result of personal failure. Pain, in fact, can be one of the tools God uses to mold your character and change your life.

What are you to do when you are hit full-speed by the awful pain that seems to choke the very will to live out of you? Where is your consolation, your comfort, and your help?

In almighty God, whose love will never fail. When life knocks you to your knees, you're closer to God than ever before.

It's a mess. Went from a one-and-a-half week deal to six. It's a nuisance.
— Mike Leach on his midseason injury

**When life hits you with pain, you can always
turn to God for comfort, consolation, and hope.**

THE CHALLENGE

Read Matthew 4:12-25.

"Come, follow me," Jesus said (v. 19).

Playing major college basketball presented a special and unique challenge for Tech's Luke Adams: He is deaf.

Adams' size left him with quite enough of a challenge in his dream to play major college basketball. He stood only 5'9" tall and weighed in at a less-than-hulking 150 pounds, not exactly the ideal size college coaches look for.

Thus, despite a senior season in which he averaged 26.9 points per game, Adams drew interest from only a few smaller four-year schools and some junior colleges. Relying on his faith, he decided to walk on at Texas Tech. "I prayed about it," he said, "so I think God showed me that this was the place I needed to go."

Adams faced the daunting challenges common to all walk-ons at a major school. In his case, though, there was more; Adams was born deaf. "When I grew up, I never saw myself as different," he said about always trying to maintain what he called a normal life-style. "I never felt really sorry for myself either."

Adams not only made the team as a freshman in 2011-12, but played in 23 games and started seven of them. When he finished up in 2014-15, he had appeared in 59 games.

Adams has a cochlear implant and hearing aids, but playing basketball still presented special challenges for him because he doesn't hear as well as everyone else does. "Being on the court,

I use my eyes more than most people do," he said. "I try to look around any time there is a dead ball. . . . I'm always looking at [the head coach]. I've just got to use my eyes to hear."

"He's the toughest guy on our team," head coach Billy Gillispie said of Adams his freshman season. "He was dealt a tough blow, but he's never let that affect him." Except to make him more determined to meet life's challenges.

Like Luke Adams every time he took the court for the Red Raiders, we are challenged daily. Life is a testing ground; God intentionally set it up that way. If we are to grow in character, confidence, and perseverance, and if we are to make a difference in the world, we must meet challenges head-on. Few things in life are as boring and as destructive to our sense of self-worth as a job that doesn't offer any challenges.

Our faith life is the same way. The moment we answered Jesus' call to "Come, follow me," we took on the most difficult challenge we will ever face. We are called to be holy by walking in Jesus' footsteps in a world that seeks to render our Lord irrelevant and his influence negligible. The challenge Jesus places before us is to put our faith and our trust in him and not in ourselves or the transitory values of the secular world.

Daily walking in Jesus' footsteps is a challenge, but the path takes us all the way right up to the gates of Heaven — and then right on through.

I like the challenge.
— *Luke Adams on being a walk-on at Texas Tech*

To accept Jesus as Lord is to joyfully take on the challenge of living a holy life in an unholy world.

DAY 17

STAR POWER

Read Luke 10:1-3, 17-20.

"The Lord appointed seventy-two others and sent them two by two ahead of him to every town and place where he was about to go" (v. 1).

Of all the stars that Texas Tech football has showcased over the decades, perhaps the most unlikely of them all was Wes Welker.

Simply put, Welker was too short and too slow to be a major college football player, let alone a star. He was from Oklahoma City, but Oklahoma didn't want him. Oklahoma State said they'd let him walk on. Tulsa offered him a scholarship and then backed off. So in 1999, two weeks after signing day was over and done with, Welker and his family drove to Lubbock.

Welker told first-year Tech coach Mike Leach and his staff, "I want to play for you," but he would walk on at Oklahoma State if he couldn't get a scholarship. If Tech made him an offer, he said, "I'll be here as soon as school's out and be ready to play for the season." He left a tape behind while he toured the Tech campus with one of the strength coaches.

"It was the most impressive high school film I've ever seen," Leach declared. "He did everything. His production was off the scale." The decision was made to offer Welker a scholarship.

Quarterback Kliff Kingsbury was like everyone else when he first saw Welker at practice. "Oh my gosh, who is this little frat guy?" he thought. By the end of that initial practice, Kingsbury's thinking was "This guy is our best player."

Welker's "last-minute signing proved to be a bonanza" for the Red Raiders. He was a four-year starter who caught 259 passes for 21 TDs and rushed for 456 yards. He set an NCAA record with eight punt returns for touchdowns. As a senior, he won the Mosi Tatupu Award as the top special teams player in the country.

Football teams are like other organizations in that they may have a star such as Wes Welker, but the star would be nothing without the supporting cast. It's the same in a private company, in a government bureaucracy, in a military unit, and just about any other team of people with a common goal.

That includes the team known as a church. It may have its "star" in the pastor, who is — like the quarterback or the company CEO — the most visible representative of the team. Preachers are, after all, God's anointed, paid, and trained professionals.

But when Jesus rounded up a team of seventy-two folks and sent them out, he didn't have any experienced evangelists or any educated seminary graduates on his payroll. All he had was a bunch of no-names who loved him. Centuries later, nothing has changed. God's church still depends on those whose only pay is the satisfaction of serving and whose only qualification is their abiding love for God. God's church needs you.

Wes Welker is one of the most accomplished players ever to suit up for Texas Tech.

— Rana L. Cash of Sporting News

Yes, the church needs its professional clergy, but it also needs those who serve as volunteers because they love God; the church needs you.

DAY 18

WHO, ME?

Read Judges 6:11-23.

"'But Lord,' Gideon asked, 'how can I save Israel? My clan is the weakest in Manasseh, and I am the least in my family'" (v. 15).

A former walk-on unexpectedly came off the bench to play a key role in Tech's 70-57 upset of top-ranked and undefeated Louisville at Madison Square Garden on Dec. 10, 2019.

Tech lost four of its top five scorers off the miracle team of 2018-19 that took Virginia into overtime in the national championship game before losing. Thus, it really wasn't surprising when the Raiders suffered a three-game losing streak early in the 2019-20 season.

But when they arrived in New York City for the showdown with the Cardinals, the Red Raiders were even more shorthanded. Leading scorer Jahmi'us Ramsey was sidelined by a hamstring injury for the third straight game.

Junior point guard and returning starter Davide Moretti, who was third-team All-Big 12 in 2019, did his part. He scored 18 points and buried two straight threes midway through the second half that propelled Tech into an 11-point lead. Louisville never made a run after that.

But an unlikely player also played a big part in the huge upset. That would be "scruffy walk-on Avery Benson." His line score was pretty good. In 22 minutes on the court, he scored ten points with perfect shooting from the field and the free-throw line. He also had four rebounds.

But it was what Benson did to the fans and his teammates that was his biggest contribution. He had a pair of "highlight-reel blocks" that stunned the Cards in the first half. They also drove the already frenetic Tech crowd into a complete and total frenzy.

Described as a "shaggy-haired, ink-stained bundle of energy," Benson used that energy to fire up his teammates from the tip.

You've probably experienced a "Who, Me?" moment or two in your life. Perhaps yours wasn't as pleasant as Avery Benson's taking command of the crowd at Madison Square Garden, but was a moment of unwelcome surprise with its concomitant sinking feeling. Maybe you've had to testify in court. Or had to deliver tragic news to the other members of your family. You've suffered that turmoil in your midsection when you found yourself in a situation you neither sought nor were totally prepared for.

You may feel exactly as Gideon did about being called to serve God in some way. You quail at the very notion of being audacious enough to teach Sunday school, coordinate a high school prayer club, or lead a small group study. Who, me? Hey, who's worthy enough to do anything like that?

The truth is that nobody is — but that doesn't seem to matter to God. And it's his opinion, not yours, that counts.

Sometimes, it's hard to pump the brakes, but I'd rather pump the brakes than not be rolling at all.
— Avery Benson on riling up fans and players alike at the Garden

**You're right in that no one is worthy to serve God,
but that doesn't matter to God.**

DAY 19

CHANGEOVER

Read Romans 6:1-14.

"Just as Christ was raised from the dead through the glory of the Father, we too may live a new life" (v. 4).

A severe neck injury forced Donny Anderson to change the way he played football. He thus became a Texas Tech legend.

Guy Griffis, a Tech safety and Anderson's roommate in 1965, said, "Donny Anderson put Tech on the map." He was an All-American running back in both 1964 and '65 and was three times named All-Southwest Conference. He finished fourth in the Heisman voting in '65, was one of the first three players inducted into the Texas Tech Ring of Honor, and had his jersey (no. 44) retired in 1995. He was inducted into the College Football Hall of Fame in 1989.

Anderson's time as an all-state running back and linebacker in high school came to an inglorious end when he suffered a neck injury making a tackle. One of Anderson's coaches said his star "basically had a broken neck," but the injury was not career threatening. It did, however, force Anderson to make some changes in his game.

He admitted that he was no longer as aggressive on the field as he had been. He worked on his speed and "became more of a finesse player, shifty, instinctive."

Still, Tech head coach JT King (1961-69) recruited Anderson as a linebacker rather than a running back. That changed when

King was in the press box one day watching a freshman game. Anderson was playing both ways, and on offense he touched the ball nine times and scored five touchdowns. King called down to freshman coach Burl Huffman and said. "Before we move that boy back to linebacker, let's see him run a few more times."

Donny Anderson's days as a finesse running back rather than a tough linebacker had begun. His achievements helped change the perception of Texas Tech football, legitimizing the conference's newest kid on the block. (Tech had joined in 1960.)

Anyone who asserts no change is needed in his or her life just isn't paying attention. Every life has doubt, worry, fear, failure, frustration, unfulfilled dreams, and unsuccessful relationships in some combination. The memory and consequences of our past often haunt and trouble us.

Simply recognizing the need for change in our lives, though, doesn't mean the changes that will bring about hope, joy, peace, and fulfillment will occur. We need some power greater than ourselves or we wouldn't be where we are.

So where can we turn to? Where lies the hope for a changed life? It lies in an encounter with the Lord of all Hope: Jesus Christ. For a life turned over to Jesus, change is inevitable. With Jesus in charge, the old self with its painful and destructive ways of thinking, feeling, loving, and living is transformed.

A changed life is always only a talk with Jesus away.

Until [his injury], the defining thing for me about Donny was his toughness. At Tech, he became more of a finesse player.
— *High school coach Clint Ramsey*

In Jesus lies the power that changes lives.

DAY 20

FAMILY TIES

Read Mark 3:31-35.

"[Jesus] said, 'Here are my mother and my brothers!
Whoever does God's will is my brother and sister and
mother'" (vv. 34-35).

Casey Morris left one family and traveled more than 1,300 miles to find another.

Basketball early on was a family affair for Morris. Her dad, Charles, introduced her to the game when she was a youngster. In the Air Force, he played and coached every chance he got. "I played for his team when I was little," she remembered. "And I have just loved [basketball] ever since."

As Morris grew up, basketball was always a part of her life, first on a club team and then in high school. Recruited heavily as a senior in 2008, she opted for her family, choosing to play for California, her mother's alma mater. The school was close to her home, so she could visit family whenever she wanted.

Morris played every game her freshman year; the team did very well, making the NCAA's Sweet 16. Still, something wasn't right for Morris. She just didn't fit in, and she decided to transfer. She had a school in mind, even though it was more than 1,300 miles from her California home. That school was Texas Tech.

Morris had a connection with Tech in that her dad had once been stationed near Lubbock. The coaching staff had come to California to recruit her when she was in high school, and she had liked them. "They were just loyal," she said. So she packed her bags and headed to Texas to play for Kristy Curry.

In Lubbock, Morris found herself a member of a new family, declaring she had never been on a team with such a close bond. The fit was a good one for her, and it showed in her game. After sitting out a season because of her transfer, Morris was a three-year starter at guard. Her senior season of 2012-13, she earned All-Big 12 Second-Team honors. She was the second-leading scorer as the team won 21 games and made it to the Big Dance.

Some wit said families are like fudge, mostly sweet with a few nuts. You can probably call the names of your sweetest relatives, whom you cherish, and of the nutty ones too, whom you mostly try to avoid at a family reunion.

Whether you like it or not, you have a family just as Casey Morris does. That's God's doing. God cherishes the family so much that he chose to live in one as a son, a brother, and a cousin.

One of Jesus' more startling actions was to redefine the family. No longer is it a single household of blood relatives or even a clan or a tribe. Jesus' family is the result, not of an accident of birth, but rather a conscious choice. All those who do God's will are members of Jesus' family.

What a startling and downright wonderful thought! You have family members out there you don't even know who stand ready to love you just because you're part of God's family.

I feel like we are all family. We are all sisters.
— Casey Morris on her Lady Raider teammates

For followers of Jesus, family comes not from
a shared ancestry but from a shared faith.

DAY 21

THE NIGHTMARE

Read Mark 5:1-20.

"What do you want with me, Jesus, Son of the Most High God? Swear to God that you won't torture me!" (v. 7)

Sammy Morris was Texas A&M's worst nightmare.

Morris lettered only twice for the Red Raiders, but that didn't keep him from terrorizing the Aggies in 1996 and 1999.

In practice the week of the '96 A&M game, offensive coordinator Rick Dykes put in a play designed to get Morris open out of the backfield. He called it "Aggie Touchdown."

Tech trailed 10-6 late when A&M called a timeout. Quarterback Zebbie Lethridge trotted to the sideline, took the headset, and got the call from Dykes he expected. "I thought you might say that," he replied when Dykes called for "Aggie Touchdown."

The Raiders stationed three receivers to the tight side of the field, decoys to pull coverage away from Morris. On the other side, they faked a run directly at the cornerback. Meanwhile, Morris circled out and up the sideline behind that cornerback. "He wound up far up the field with seemingly no maroon jersey in his ZIP code." He was so open all he had to do was avoid dropping the pass.

"Aggie Touchdown" went for 81 yards and a 13-10 Tech win. In the coaches' box upstairs, receivers coach David Moody was so excited that when he grabbed and hugged Dykes, he broke the coordinator's glasses, which cut his face.

Morris was back in 1999, and again the Red Raiders had a nightmarish surprise in store for A&M. An injury sidelined the regular tailback, Ricky Williams, so the coaches moved Morris from fullback. He ran the ball 33 times for 170 yards in a 21-19 upset of the fifth-ranked Aggies.

"We thought we could run the ball right at them. . . . Sammy was physical enough we thought he could get the tough yards inside the tackles, and he did," said Dykes, explaining how it was that Morris could once again be the Aggies' worst nightmare.

Falling. Drowning. Standing naked in a room crowded with fully dressed people. They're nightmares, dreams that jolt us from our sleep in anxiety or downright terror. The film industry has used our common nightmares to create horror movies that allow us to experience our fears vicariously. This includes the formulaic "evil vs. good" movies in which demons and the like render good virtually helpless in the face of their power and ruthlessness.

The spiritual truth, though, is that it is evil that has come face to face with its worst nightmare in Jesus. We seem to understand that our basic mission as Jesus' followers is to further his kingdom and change the world through emulating him in the way we live and love others. But do we appreciate that in truly living for Jesus, we are daily tormenting the very devil himself?

Satan and his lackeys quake helplessly in fear before the power of almighty God that is in us through Jesus.

[Sammy] Morris made sure to torture Texas A&M both seasons.
— Sportswriter Don Williams

As the followers of Jesus Christ,
we are the stuff of Satan's nightmares.

DAY 22

JUGGERNAUT

Read Revelation 20.

"Fire came down from heaven and devoured them. And the devil, who deceived them, was thrown into the lake of burning sulfur, where the beast and the false prophet had been thrown" (vv. 9b-10a).

The Red Raiders once unleashed a juggernaut on the unsuspecting Baylor Bears the likes of which Tech fans had not seen for decades — if ever.

The 3-3 Raiders were favored over the 2-4 Bears in Waco on Oct. 27, 2001, but what happened was unexpected. Tech demolished Baylor 63-19 and the game wasn't that close.

Tech scored on its first four possessions with running back Ricky Williams getting TDs on runs of 2, 37, and 5 yards. Quarterback Kliff Kingsbury notched the fourth touchdown with a 33-yard completion to wide receiver Carlos Francis.

Meanwhile, the Tech defense forced Baylor into three-and-out on its first four possessions. The Bears didn't make a first down until the second quarter.

An interception by two-time All-American cornerback Kevin Curtis set up another TD, and safety Ryan Aycock took a theft 19 yards to score. When the Baylor kicker bobbled a punt snap, safety Paul McClendon took the loose ball in for six more points.

That made it 49-0 — in the first half!

The Raiders cruised after that. Kingsbury was on the bench

with his helmet off before the third quarter ended. Williams went for 153-yards and a career-best four touchdowns.

The rout sent historians scrambling to the record books. The Raiders started playing football in 1925; these were the most points they had ever scored in a road game and the most points they had ever scored in the sixty meetings between the two teams. The 63 points were also the most Tech had ever scored in a Big 12 Conference game.

The steamrolled Bears just never knew what hit them.

Maybe your experience with a juggernaut involved a game against a team full of major college prospects, a league tennis match against a former college player, or your presentation for the project you knew didn't stand a chance. Whatever it was, you've been slam-dunked before.

Being part of a juggernaut is much more fun than being in the way of one. Just ask Baylor after that 2001 Tech game. Or consider the forces of evil aligned against God. At least the Bears had a shot at winning when they took the field against the Red Raiders. No such hope exists for those who oppose God.

That's because their fate is already spelled out in detail. It's in the book; we all know how the story ends. God's enemies may talk big and bluster now, but they will be soundly trounced and routed in the most decisive defeat of all time.

You sure want to be on the winning side in that one.

We came out and executed well early and it just snowballed from there.
— Kliff Kingsbury on the '01 Baylor game

The most lopsided victory in all of history
will be God's ultimate triumph over evil.

DAY 23

BONE TIRED

Read Matthew 11:27-30.

"Come to me, all you who are weary and burdened, and I will give you rest" (v. 11).

The Texas Tech defense was exhausted. Nevertheless, it had enough in the tank to make one last stand and preserve an overtime win over Nebraska.

The seventh-ranked Red Raiders were undefeated when the Cornhuskers came to town on Oct. 11, 2008. The defense had held its last three opponents to fewer than 300 yards and less than 30 minutes of possession time. On this day, though, that defense found itself pushed around the whole game by the Husker offense.

When the fourth quarter ended, Nebraska had controlled the ball for 40:12 and had generated more than 400 yards of offense, scoring twice in the last period to tie the game at 31. The good news for the defense was the Huskers hadn't won the game; the bad news was the game wasn't over.

"It doesn't matter how long we're on the field," declared middle linebacker Brian Duncan, the team's leading tackler. "It's all about, 'We started it and we're going to finish it.'"

On the first play of overtime, running back Baron Batch took a screen pass from Graham Harrell 24 yards to the 1. Eric Morris punched it in from there. Then to the Raiders' horror, Nebraska blocked the extra point, leaving the gate open for a Tech loss.

But the tired defense rose up. On Nebraska's second play, end

McKinner Dixon pressured the Husker quarterback into trying to throw the ball out of bounds. Instead, it sailed right to cornerback Jamar Wall. He bobbled the ball at first but then gathered it in and bolted to the Tech sideline. There he was mobbed by his teammates, including his overworked defensive compadres, who had had enough left to preserve a 37-31 win.

The everyday struggles and burdens of life beat us down. They may be enormous; they may be trivial with a cumulative effect. But they wear us out, so much so that we've even come up with a name for our exhaustion: chronic fatigue syndrome.

Doctors don't help too much. Sleeping pills can zonk us out; muscle relaxers can dull the weariness. Other than that, it's drag on as usual until we can collapse exhaustedly into bed.

Then along comes Jesus, as usual offering hope and relief for what ails us, though in a totally unexpected way. He says take my yoke. Whoa, there! Isn't a yoke a device for work? Exactly.

The mistake we all too often make lies in trying to do it alone. We rely on ourselves instead of Jesus. If we yoke ourselves to our Lord, the unimaginable, limitless power of almighty God is at our disposal to do the heavy lifting for us.

God's strong shoulders and broad back can handle any burdens we can give him. We just have to let them go.

You're always going to be out of gas. You get that extra amount of energy, and you know that you have to do it from there.
— *Jamar Wall on playing overtime*

Tired and weary are a way of life only when we fail to accept Jesus' invitation to swap our burden for his.

DAY 24

CONFIDENCE MAN

Read Micah 7:5-7.

"As for me, I will look to the Lord, I will wait for the God of my salvation" (v. 7 NRSV).

Zach Glavash's running career was in shambles, his confidence shattered — until his coach came up with a training technique the runner thought was crazy.

Already one of the country's best 800-meter sprinters, Glavash transferred to Tech from Illinois in 2006 to train under Tech head track and field coach Wes Kittley. He started well in 2006, winning the Big 12 indoor title in school-record time.

In the outdoor regional meet, however, Glavash was running the opening leg of Tech's 1600-meter relay team when he heard a pop and fell flat on his face. His right hamstring was torn; his junior season was over.

He worked hard and returned for his senior season. When he ran, though, he had trouble breathing from a severe pain in his throat. He eventually was diagnosed with a fungal infection that disappeared when he stopped using a new asthma inhaler.

The damage was done. Glavash's physical loss of confidence in his body turned into a mental loss of confidence in his abilities. In a California meet, he finished an-unheard-of twelfth.

He seriously considered quitting; Kittley entertained no such thoughts. "One day I just tried something different," the coach said. Kittley had Glavash run a 700-meter dash at practice under circumstances that matched those of a meet. Glavash warmed up like it was a meet, and Kittley stationed other team members along the track to cheer him on as if it were a real competition.

Glavash first looked at his coach as though he were crazy. "I told him to trust me," Kittley said. He did and ran one of his fastest 700 meters. His confidence restored by the unusual technique, Glavash won the Big 12 800-meter dash, finished second in the Midwest Regional, and advanced all the way to the NCAA semi-finals before his season ended.

You need confidence in all areas of your life. You're confident the company you work for will pay you on time, or you wouldn't go to work. You turn the ignition confident your car will start. When you flip a switch, you expect the light to come on.

Confidence in other people and in things is often misplaced, though. Companies go broke; car batteries die; light bulbs burn out. Even the people you love the most sometimes let you down.

So where can you place your trust with absolute confidence that you won't be betrayed? In the promises of God.

Such confidence is easy, of course, when everything's going your way, but what about when you cry as Micah did, "What misery is mine!" As Micah declared, that's the time in your life when your confidence in God must be its strongest. That's when you wait for the Lord confident that God will not fail you, that he will never let you down.

My confidence was down, and I didn't know if I could do this anymore.
— Zach Glavash in the wake of his injury

People, things, and organizations will let you down; only God can be trusted confidently.

DAY 25

PAY YOUR RESPECTS

Read Mark 8:31-38.

"He then began to teach them that the Son of Man must suffer many things and be rejected by the elders, chief priests and teachers of the law, and that he must be killed" (v. 31).

Heading into the 2013 Holiday Bowl, the Red Raiders got no respect; it all went to Arizona State. Boy, did that ever change.

The publicity and hoopla before the game in San Diego on Dec. 30 was so one-sided that Tech head coach Kliff Kingsbury called it "a celebration of Arizona State." Then, he admitted, "It should have been." That's because the Sun Devils went into the game as the champs of the Pac 12's South Division. They had closed the regular season with seven straight wins before losing the league championship game to Stanford. The Red Devils, on the other hand, had ended the season with a miserable five-game losing streak; only one of the games was close.

Thus, Arizona State was a 14-point favorite. Some pundits said they'd win by as much as 22. "We knew what people thought and we knew the type of team we had," Kingsbury said. "So we used that to fuel the fire."

And one heck of a fire it turned out to be.

Freshman quarterback Davis Webb got the start and made Holiday Bowl history. He threw for 403 yards and four touchdowns, the latter the bowl's record. Sophomore wide receiver Jakeem

Grant caught two of them with junior running back Rodney Hall and senior wide receiver Bradley Marquez snatching the other two scores. The Red Raiders scored on four of their first five possessions and jumped out to a 27-6 lead only five minutes into the second quarter. Arizona State could never recover as Tech went on to win 37-23, the output 18 points below State's season average.

"They were the more passionate team today," declared State head coach Todd Graham. "Give them credit. They came to play."

And to earn a little respect along the way.

Rodney Dangerfield made a good living with a comedic repertoire that was basically only countless variations on one punch line: "I don't get no respect." Dangerfield was successful because he struck a chord with his audience. Like the late comedian, we all seek a measure of respect in our lives. We want the respect, the esteem, and the regard we feel we have earned..

But more often than not we don't get it. Still, we shouldn't feel too badly; we're in good company. In the ultimate example of disrespect, Jesus — the Son of God — was treated as the worst type of criminal. He was arrested, bound, scorned, ridiculed, spit upon, tortured, condemned, and executed.

God allowed his son to undergo such treatment because of his high regard and his love for each one of us. We are respected by almighty God! Could anyone else's respect really matter?

We didn't get any respect all weekend long.
— Red Raider wide receiver Eric Ward on the Holiday Bowl

You may not get the respect you deserve,
but at least nobody's spitting on you
and driving nails into you as they did to Jesus.

DAY 26

DANCING MACHINE

Read 2 Samuel 6:12-22.

"David danced before the Lord with all his might, while he and the entire house of Israel brought up the ark of the Lord with shouts and the sound of trumpets" (vv. 14-15).

A thorough whipping of Oklahoma had the Red Raiders dancing — except for head coach Mike Leach.

In 2008, the Raiders could only stand and listen to some especially galling music late in an embarrassing loss to the Sooners in Norman. OU players and fans celebrated the win by dancing to the tune of House of Pain's "Jump Around."

As if that weren't enough to sour the players on the music, they heard it repeatedly once they returned to Lubbock. "All year, they had been playing it in the weight room," junior cornerback LaRon Moore said. "Nobody really liked that song. They would play it, and it would remind us of OU."

Thus, when the Raiders welcomed Oklahoma to Lubbock on Nov. 21, 2009, they had payback on their minds — and they got it in a big way. From start to finish, Tech ran all over the Sooners in an epic 41-13 beatdown that was Leach's 83rd win as the head Raider, a school record. "They just kicked our butts. That's all you can say," declared a refreshingly honest OU defensive end.

Then early in the fourth quarter, "with Tech laying the wood to Oklahoma," the stadium's public address system suddenly broke into "Jump Around." The players responded immediately as "the sideline resembled [the] dance floor of *American Bandstand*."

Leach said the song, which played three times, wasn't his idea. "I'm not a huge jump around guy," he declaimed. Even defensive coordinator Ruffin McNeill couldn't resist the music, bobbing his head gently and rhythmically. Practically everyone else on the sideline "got up, got down, kicked it out, [and] hopped around."

In celebration, the Raiders danced to the music.

One of the more enduring stereotypes of the Christian is of a dour, sour-faced person always on the prowl to sniff out fun and frivolity and shut it down. "Somewhere, sometime, somebody's having fun — and it's got to stop!" Many understand this to be the mandate that governs the Christian life.

But nothing could be further from reality or the truth. Ages ago King David, he who would eventually number Jesus Christ among his house and lineage, set the standard for those who love and worship the Lord when he danced in the presence of God with unrestrained joy. Many centuries and one savior later, David's example reminds us today that a life spent in an awareness of God's presence is all about celebrating, rejoicing, and enjoying God's countless gifts, including salvation in Jesus Christ.

Yes, dancing can be vulgar and coarse, but as with David, God looks into our hearts to see what is there. Our very life should be one long song and dance for Jesus.

I was too self-conscious to dance, really.
— Mike Leach on responding to 'Jump Around'

While dancing and music can be vulgar and obscene, they can also be inspiring expressions of abiding love for God.

DAY 27

THE FALL

Read Genesis 3:1-7, 21-24.

"When the woman saw that the fruit of the tree was good . . . , she took some and ate it. She also gave some to her husband" (v.6).

Texas Tech's excitable head football coach once fell so hard and so far during a game that some of the players thought he had killed himself.

From 1930-40, Pete Cawthon led the Red Raiders into their first golden era. His tenure included the program's first ten-win seasons and its first bowl trips. In Cawthon's case, the gruff demeanor of a drill sergeant couldn't hide "a sympathetic, God-fearing, hard-driving man who earned the everlasting love and respect of 'his boys.'"

Cawthon hated to lose so badly that he was known "to hibernate for hours or even days after losing a 'close one.'" More than once, when his team lost another of those close ones, he waited for the fans to clear the stadium and then sent the players back out for a two-hour practice.

Not surprisingly, therefore, Cawthon was anything but stoic on the sideline. He usually sat on a medicine box during a game and had the rather unfortunate habit of throwing his arms into the air when something on the field didn't suit him. This invariably caused him to fall over backwards, but since the box was so small, he was never injured.

One time, though, he perched himself on a large steamer trunk used to carry the team's headgear. Sure enough, during the game Cawthon showed his disgust in his usual manner. He threw his arms into the air and promptly tumbled over backwards. He wasn't on that little medicine box, though, and "with arms flailing, [he] toppled about four feet to the ground."

Some of the players were sure the fall had killed him. It didn't.

We live in a fallen world, which is the Christian faith's short-hand way of saying that neither we nor the planet itself are what they were when God created them. Disobedience to God effected the change and brought both sin and evil into the world. They've never left, in large part because we continue to repeat Adam and Eve's original misstep.

That is, as the first twosome did, we desire to be like God (v. 5). Even more arrogantly, we want to *be* God. So we claim autonomy, supplant God's rules with our own, seek out the forbidden, and generally deny God's will for our lives. We live in a state of per-petual disobedience, which, just as with Adam and Eve, results in separation from God.

This is sin, the use of our God-given freedom to assert indepen-dence from our creator. This is The Fall; we have lost the Garden. Through God's awesome grace, though, we have a way back to the Garden and to righteousness. Jesus Christ is that way.

We all thought he had killed himself, but we were all afraid to go over and see if he was all right.
    — Dudley Aiken on Pete Cawthon's fall from the steamer trunk

The Fall brought sin and death to the creation;
Jesus brings righteousness and life to it.

THE LEADER

Read Matthew 16:13-19.

"You are Peter, and on this rock I will build my church, and the gates of Hades will not overcome it" (v. 18).

With the departure of Dakota Allen (NFL draft), who senior offensive lineman Travis Bruffy called "the best leader I've ever been around," the 2019 Red Raiders needed someone to step up. Senior linebacker Jordyn Brooks did just that, becoming a leader both on the field and in the locker room.

Brooks finished his career in 2019 with 367 career tackles, the seventh-best total in school history. He was named First-Team All-Big 12 and a Second-Team All American.

His astounding performance in the 45-35 upset of 21st-ranked Oklahoma State on Oct. 5 established him as the on-field leader. He recorded 19 tackles, including four for loss, three sacks and one quarterback hit and forced a fumble. An amazed defensive coordinator Keith Patterson said Brooks recorded 56 points on the production board, the most points he had ever seen a linebacker put up in more than 20 years of using the board.

But Brooks also assumed the role of a team leader off the field. Bruffy called him "one of the biggest leaders on the team. [He] "stepped into the role seamlessly."

Following the loss to Oklahoma on Sept. 28, the Raiders held a team meeting with Brooks no doubt taking a leader's role. "He is at the forefront of every positive change that this program is experiencing," Bruffy said of Brooks. "He takes all the responsibility, good and bad."

For Brooks, with the mantle of leadership came the responsibility of working harder. Defensive back Douglas Coleman III said Brooks' success stemmed from his work ethic. Working hard "is just something I like to take pride in," Brooks the leader said.

Every aspect of life that involves people – every organization, every group, every team -- must have a leader. If goals are to be reached, somebody like Jordyn Brooks must take charge.

Even the early Christian church was no different. Jesus knew this, so he designated the leader in Simon Peter, who was such an unlikely choice to assume such an awesome, world-changing responsibility that Jesus soon after rebuked him as "Satan."

In *Twelve Ordinary Men*, John MacArthur described Simon as "ambivalent, vacillating, impulsive, unsubmissive." Hardly a man to inspire confidence in his leadership skills. Yet, according to MacArthur, Peter became "the greatest preacher among the apostles" and the "dominant figure" in the birth of the church.

The implication for your own life is both obvious and unsettling. You may think you lack the attributes necessary to make a good leader for Christ. But consider Simon Peter, an ordinary man who allowed Christ to rule his life and became the foundation upon which the Christian church was built.

The best leaders are following Christ. That's the best leader you can follow.

— Former NFL head coach Tony Dungy

**God's leaders are men and women
who allow Jesus to lead them.**

DAY 29

GOD'S CONQUERORS

Read John 16:19-33.

"In this world you will have trouble. But take heart! I have overcome the world" (v. 33b).

The Raiders set school and Big 12 records on offense, but still had much to overcome to win the game. Mostly, they had to overcome themselves.

On Sept. 27, 2003, Tech put on a dazzling display against Ole Miss in Oxford. Quarterback B.J. Symons set school and conference records by completing 44 of 64 passes for a mind-boggling 661 yards. His 681 yards of total offense was the third highest in major college football history as he outdueled Eli Manning.

Thus, the Rebel defense was pretty much helpless against the Tech offense, which set a school record with 713 total yards. Or so it seemed. In fact, four Tech turnovers not only kept Ole Miss in the game but put Tech in such a deep hole that only a late two-touchdown rally pulled out the 49-45 win.

Turnovers by the offense and breakdowns by special teams almost negated all that yardage. A comfortable 21-10 Tech lead in the first half transformed into a 32-21 deficit in the third quarter. The 11-point gap held up deep into the fourth quarter as Ole Miss led 45-34. "I was never worried, because our offense was just hurting ourselves," Symons said.

A 21-yard TD pass to freshman Jarrett Hicks, who would finish up as one of Tech's greatest receivers, and a two-point conversion toss to junior H-back Clay McGuire with 5 minutes to play got Tech close at 45-42.

After a Rebel punt, Symons and receivers Mickey Peters and Wes Welker led the offense on a 67-yard drive. The game winner came on a 9-yard toss to senior Carlos Francis with 1:04 left. It was Symons' sixth TD toss of the game, and Tech needed every one of them to overcome its mistakes and win.

We each have a choice to make about how we live. We can merely survive or we can overcome as Tech did against Ole Miss.

We often hear inspiring stories of people who triumph by overcoming especially daunting obstacles. Those barriers may be physical or mental disabilities, or great personal tragedies, or injustice. When we hear of them, we may well respond with a little prayer of thanksgiving that life has been kinder to us.

But all people of faith, no matter how drastic the obstacles they face, must ultimately overcome the same opponent: the Satan-infested world. Some do have it tougher than others, but we all must fight daily to remain confident and optimistic.

To merely survive from day to day is to give up by surrendering our trust in God's involvement in our daily life. To overcome, however, is to stand up to the world and fight its temptations that would erode the armor of our faith in Jesus Christ.

Today is a day for you to overcome by remaining faithful. The very hosts of Heaven wait to hail the conquering hero.

We made some mistakes but I'm proud of the way we overcame them.
— Mike Leach on the '03 Ole Miss game

Life's difficulties provide us a chance to experience the true joy of victory in Jesus.

A FAST START

Read Acts 2:40-47.

"Everyone was filled with awe. . . . [They] ate together with glad and sincere hearts, praising God and enjoying the favor of all the people" (vv. 43a, 46b, 47a).

The schedule gave Spike Dykes the chance to get his coaching career at Texas Tech off to a fast start. Then the schedule changed.

Dykes actually coached a game before his first official season at the helm began in the fall of 1987. When David McWilliams left for Texas, Dykes took over the program and coached the team in the Independence Bowl against Ole Miss.

The '87 season, though, marked a beginning for Dykes and the coaching staff he had assembled. He liked the way the schedule looked in that his team was to open with Arkansas State, a game the Raiders should win.

During the offseason, though, Dykes and athletic director T Jones discussed their shared belief that Tech needed to beef up its schedule to upgrade the perception of the program. Early in June, Jones approached his head coach and told him he had gotten Tech out of the Arkansas State game.

"Good," Dykes replied. "Who's going to replace them?"

"Uh, we're going to Florida State," Jones answered.

Dykes agreed that going to Tallahassee certainly constituted an upgrade. The Seminoles were coming off an 11-1 season that ended with a No.-3 ranking and a win in the Sugar Bowl.

RED RAIDERS

Dykes' hopes for a fast start took another blow when quarterback Billy Joe Tolliver sprained his ankle at practice the Thursday before the game. That thrust Scott Toman, who had never taken a snap for Tech, into the start. "All he did," Dykes said, "was play one of the most phenomenal games."

The final score of 40-16 doesn't show it, but Dykes' team did get off to a fast start toward changing the program's perception. Tech battled FSU, which would finish No. 2 in the nation, to a 30-16 halftime score before the Noles pulled away the last half.

Fast starts are crucial for more than football games and races. Any time we begin something new, we want to get out of the gate quickly, build up momentum from a fast start, and keep rolling.

This is true for our faith life also. For a time after we accepted Christ as our savior, we were on fire with a zeal that wouldn't let us rest, much like the early Christians described in Acts. All too many Christians, however, let that blaze die down until only old ashes remain. We become lukewarm pew sitters.

The Christian life shouldn't be that way. Just because we were tepid yesterday doesn't mean we can't be boiling today. Every day we can turn to God for a spiritual tune-up that will put a new spark in our faith life; with a little tending, that spark can soon become a raging fire. Today could be the day our faith life gets off to a fast start — again.

We needed to develop the mindset that we were eager to face anybody, anywhere at any time.
— Athletic director T Jones on the decision to play FSU in '87

**Every day offers us yet another chance
to get off to a fast start for Jesus.**

DAY 31

BEING DIFFERENT

Read Daniel 3.

"We want you to know, O king, that we will not serve your gods or worship the image of gold you have set up" (v. 18).

In 1996, Darvin Ham became the first Texas Tech athlete to be featured on the cover of *Sports Illustrated*, but it was for something different he did on the court.

From 1993-96, Ham, a 6-7 forward, played in 90 games for the Raiders, averaging 8.1 points and 5.1 rebounds per game. He was a senior on the 1995-96 team led by Third-Team All-American Jason Sasser that went 30-2, was undefeated in the Southwest Conference, and advanced to the Sweet 16 in the NCAA Tournament.

Whatever else Ham could do on the basketball court, he could dunk. He was credited officially with 116 dunks at Tech, though he has disputed that number, asserting it is too low. A dunk he pulled off in that '96 NCAA Tournament merited the *SI* cover.

With 12:06 left in the first half of the game against North Carolina in the round of thirty-two, Sasser missed a hook shot. Ham went up for the put-back, but he didn't just gently tap it in. Rather, he slammed the ball through the net with such power that it shattered the backboard. At the time, this was something totally different for fans; no one had ever before destroyed a backboard in the NCAA Tournament.

The packed Georgia Dome suddenly grew quiet. "The silence

in the dome that day was amazing," said Bob Bockrath, Tech's athletic director at the time. "Even the North Carolina fans were dumb struck."

Ham later said the dunk didn't even rank in his top-10 all-time, but *Sports Illustrated* made sure it became part of Tech lore. The cover showed Ham coming down with glass raining all around him. The headline simply said "Smashing!" (Tech won 92-73.)

Darvin Ham's game was different from most; Christians know all about being different. While we live in a secular society that constantly pressures us to conform to its principles and values, we serve a risen Christ who calls us to be different. Therein lies the great conflict of the Christian life in contemporary America.

But how many of us really consider that even in our secular society we struggle to conform? We are all geeks in a sense. We can never truly conform because we were not created by God to live in such a sin-filled world in the first place. Thus, when Christ calls us to be different by following and espousing Christian beliefs, principles, and practices, he is summoning us to the lifestyle we were born for.

The most important step in being different for Jesus is realizing and admitting what we really are: We are children of God; we are Christians. Only secondarily are we citizens of a secular world. That world both scorns and disdains us for being different; Jesus both praises and loves us for it.

It was just an ordinary dunk with extra power.
— Darvin Ham on his glass-shattering dunk

The lifestyle Jesus calls us to is different from that of the world, but it is the way we were born to live.

PRECIOUS MEMORIES

Read 1 Thessalonians 3:6-13.

"Timothy . . . has brought good news about your faith and love. He has told us that you always have pleasant memories of us" (v. 6).

If college football coaches are remembered fondly, it is usually because of their won-loss record. That is not the case, however, with Tech's DeWitt Weaver.

Head coach Dell Morgan resigned during the last game of the 1950 season. Prior to that game, Morgan left a sealed envelope announcing his resignation with the radio station broadcasting the game. He left instructions for its contents to be read over the air with three minutes left to play, which was done.

The search for a replacement didn't go smoothly. After a number of interviews, the school's president and the athletic council realized that they could not lure a big-name coach to Lubbock. They began to target young coaches, and eventually they called Weaver, who was an assistant at Tulsa, to come for an interview. They hired him, and he doubled up as the athletic director.

Weaver's ten-year tenure yielded a record of only 49-51-5, but he is remembered for much more than that tally. As he prepared his team for the Gator Bowl of Jan. 1, 1954, the head coach had an inspiration. He decided Texas Tech needed an immediately recognizable and exciting symbol. Thus was born the Masked Rider. (See Devotion No. 53.)

Following the 1955 season, however, there occurred what was called "the largest single event in the history of Tech football." From the outset, Weaver worked to gain Tech admittance into the Southwest Conference. On May 22, 1956, after more than twenty years and in large part because of Weaver's untiring efforts, that momentous goal was achieved. (See Devotion No. 10.)

Like DeWitt Weaver, who died in 1998, your whole life will one day be only a memory because you, too, will pass away. With that knowledge in hand, you can control much about your inevitable funeral. You can, for instance, select a funeral home, purchase a cemetery plot, pick out your casket or a tasteful urn, designate those who will deliver your eulogy, and make other less important decisions about your send-off.

What you cannot control about your death, however, is how you will be remembered and whether your demise will leave a gaping hole in the lives of those with whom you shared your life or a pothole that's quickly paved over. What determines whether those nice words someone will say about you are heartfelt truth or pleasant fabrications? What determines whether the tears that fall at your death result from true grief or just a sinus infection?

Love does. Just as Paul wrote, the love you give away during your life decides whether or not memories of you will be precious and pleasant.

It was an accomplishment that [makes] DeWitt Weaver one of the best known and cherished parts of Tech football history.
— *from* The Red Raiders *on getting into the Southwest Conference*

Because we remember Jesus,
God will not remember our sins.

EASY DOES IT

Read John 6:53-66.

"[M]any of his disciples said, 'This is a hard teaching. Who can accept it?' . . . [M]any of his disciples turned back and no longer followed him" (vv. 60, 66).

It was just too easy for the Missouri Tigers — at least for a while.

On Nov. 6, 2010, the 4-4 Red Raiders were underdogs at home to the 14th-ranked bunch from Columbia. The game was expected to be a knock-down drag-out, but in the opening minutes, two easy Missouri touchdowns showed promise of a long night for the home team. On the third play from scrimmage, the No.-4 running back on the Tigers' depth chart headed right on a sweep and zipped 69 yards for a score. Less than six minutes later, another back romped across 71 yards of real estate for another touchdown to make it 14-0 Missouri. "We had some miscommunications on the field early," said Tech defensive tackle Colby Whitlock in explaining how Missouri managed to score so easily.

From then on, though, the Tigers wound up with a whole mess of problems. "I thought the coaches did a great job of adjusting after the first couple of drives," said head coach Tommy Tuberville. Those adjustments limited Missouri to 71 yards rushing the rest of the game.

On the other side of the ball, quarterback Taylor Potts came off the bench in the second quarter to lead a Tech rally. His 16-yard pass to receiver Lyle Leong on the opening drive of the second half tied the game at 17. The game-winning drive came on Tech's next possession, which covered 85 yards. Potts and Leong again paired up for the score, this one a 5-yard chunk.

Meanwhile, nothing came easy anymore for the Tiger offense. Missouri's final three possessions totaled 13 yards, and when the clock ran out, Tech had a hard-fought 24-17 win.

Beating a tough opponent such as Missouri in football is never easy. Neither is following Jesus.

It's not just the often abstruse aspects of Jesus' teachings that test us mentally; it's that Jesus demands disruption in our lives. To take even a hesitant, tentative step toward following Jesus is to take a gigantic stride toward changing our lives — and change is never easy. In fact, we abhor it. All too often we choose to live in misery and unhappiness because it's familiar; the devil we know is better than the angel we don't.

Jesus also demands commitment. We who live in a secular, me-first age are to surrender our lives to him, to God's control. We are to think, act, live, and feel in a way totally counter to the prevailing philosophy of the world we temporarily call home. We are to keep our sights on the spiritual world, to offer up a life of service and sacrifice now in exchange for a future eternal reward.

None of that is easy. But neither was dying on a cross.

Those who truly have the spirit of champions are never wholly happy with an easy win.
> — *Swimmer and Olympic Gold medalist Nicole Haislett*

That which is easily accomplished in life
is rarely satisfying or rewarding;
this includes following Jesus.

DAY 34

THE PIONEER SPIRIT

Read Luke 5:1-11.

"So they pulled their boats up on shore, left everything and followed him" (v. 11).

Danny Hardaway was recruited by Tech for his personality and demeanor as much as for his football talent. After all, he was a pioneer.

In February 1967, Hardaway became the first African-American to sign an athletic scholarship with Texas Tech. He thus is forever part of Red Raider legend as the one who broke the color barrier.

Hardaway was well aware at the time of the significance of what he was undertaking. "I guess I was kind of anxious initially," he said. His time at Texas Tech "was different, but I was brought up an army brat. I could deal with it."

That background convinced the Tech coaches that Hardaway could handle the unique pressures on him. Plus, the coaches felt Hardaway had the perfect personality and style to fit in at Tech. He was "an affable sort" who always spoke "calmly and intelligently while focusing on the positive and ignoring the negatives."

"He was a real likable young man," remembered assistant coach John Conley, who went on to serve as Tech's athletic director from 1980-85. "He was a good guy. I'd say he handled it very well."

Hardaway experienced less overt racism than might have been expected, at least in Lubbock. "I didn't see a lot of it not in my face," he said. "But I wasn't naive. . . . I used to get some snide remarks and some racial slurs when we visited other campuses."

Recruited as a wide receiver, Hardaway was switched to running back in college. He led the team in rushing in 1969 with 483 yards, but his time at Tech didn't end well. He and first-year head coach Jim Carlen fell out in 1970, and Hardaway left Lubbock. He played his senior season at Cameron University.

Despite the unhappy ending, Hardaway, a true Texas Tech pioneer, said years later, "I'll be a Red Raider until I die."

Going to a place in your life you've never been before requires a willingness to take risks and face uncertainty head-on. You may have never broken the color barrier at a major college, but you've had your moments when your latent pioneer spirit manifested itself. That time you changed careers, ran a marathon, volunteered at a homeless shelter, or went back to school.

While attempting new things invariably begets apprehension, the truth is that when life becomes too comfortable and too familiar, it gets boring. The same is true of God, who is downright dangerous because he calls us to be anything but comfortable as we serve him. He summons us to continuously blaze new trails in our faith life, to follow him no matter what. Stepping out on faith is risky all right, but the reward is a life of accomplishment, adventure, and joy that cannot be equaled anywhere else.

There's a lot of people who got an opportunity because of the door I opened. That's one thing I'm proud of.
— Danny Hardaway on being a pioneer

**Unsafe and downright dangerous, God calls us
out of the place where we are comfortable to a life
of adventure and trailblazing in his name.**

DAY 35

PRAYER WARRIORS

Read Luke 18:1-8.

"Then Jesus told his disciples a parable to show them that they should always pray and not give up" (v. 1).

Stephanie Scott used the power of prayer to decide where she would play her college basketball.

Seven Red Raiders played every game of the 1992-93 national championship season. They came to Lubbock in different ways from different cities and towns and different backgrounds.

Noel Johnson was a four-year starter at guard who finished up as the best 3-point shooter in Southwest Conference history. Like post player Michi Atkins, a freshman on the championship team and the all-time leading scorer in SWC history, she grew up in Tech's back yard and stayed close to home. The same was true of guard Krista Kirkland, from Spearman, one of only three Lady Raiders to have her jersey retired. Forward Janice Farris, who set a Tech record for career shooting average, grew up in Lubbock and knew early on she wanted to be a Lady Raider.

Sheryl Swoopes, a collegiate and professional basketball legend and the best player on a team loaded with talent, grew up in Brownfield. She took a circuitous route to Tech, though, originally enrolling at Texas but leaving without ever touching the court. She didn't want to be that far from her family, so she played two seasons at South Plains College before transferring to Tech.

Post player Cynthia Clinger transferred from the College of

Southern Idaho despite her boyfriend's wish to go elsewhere.

And then there was Scott, who set a school record for best 3-point shooting percentage in a season. She was torn between Tech and Texas A&M. She was actually on the A&M campus when she turned to prayer to help her make a decision. She prayed for a sign, and when she raised her head, she saw a literal sign, a street sign. It was Lubbock Street. That sealed the deal for Tech.

Stephanie Scott prayed and expected an answer. That's what Jesus taught us to do: always pray and never give up.

Any problems we may have with prayer and its results derive from our side, not God's. We pray for a while about something — perhaps fervently at first — but our enthusiasm wanes if we don't receive the answer we want exactly when we want it. Why waste our time by asking for the same thing over and over again?

But God isn't deaf; God does hear our prayers, and God does respond to them. As Jesus clearly taught, our prayers have an impact because they turn the power of Almighty God loose in this world. Thus, falling to our knees and praying to God is not a sign of weakness and helplessness. Rather, praying for someone or something is an aggressive act, an intentional ministry, a conscious and fervent attempt on our part to change someone's life or the world for the better.

God responds to our prayers; we often just can't perceive or don't understand how he is working to make those prayers come about.

I prayed for a sign and I looked up and saw that sign.
— Stephanie Scott on the answer to her prayer

Jesus taught us to always pray and never give up.

DAY 36

KEEPING THE PEACE

Read Hebrews 12:14-17.

"Make every effort to live in peace with all men and to be holy" (v. 14).

At game's end, the opposing coach hurried across the field, but it sure wasn't to offer the Texas Tech head coach the traditional peace offering of a handshake.

For Red Raider strength and conditioning coach Bennie Wylie, the season-opening game against SMU on Sept. 4, 2004, included the moment in which he realized that head coach Mike Leach and his offense lacked an off switch. With only 15 seconds left to play, Tech led 27-13 and had the ball at the SMU 4-yard line. Leach called a timeout.

He then sent in a pass play, dropping quarterback Sonny Cumbie into the shotgun. Wylie could hear the furious SMU head coach screaming all the way across the field: "HIT HIM! HIT HIM! HIT THE QUARTERBACK!" Cumbie was not hit by the defense, and he threw to a wide-open receiver in the end zone, who dropped the ball.

As Wylie watched warily, the SMU head coach slammed his earphones down and followed that with his clipboard. He then started running across the field.

"I'm thinking: This is gonna be bad," Wylie later said. "He's mad at Mike for trying to score. And Mike really has no idea that he's mad. Mike is sitting there upset that we didn't score." Sure enough,

Leach wasn't even aware of the opposing coach; he was "jotting notes on his wadded-up sheet of paper with the plays on it."

So Wylie intervened and took the brunt of the coach's anger. "This guy starts poking me in the chest — Bam! Bam! Bam! — and screaming," he recalled. He let the enraged coach have his say, avoiding what very well could have turned into an ugly scene.

Perhaps you've managed to make it thus far in your life without getting involved in a brawl or a public brouhaha, whether you started it or just happened to be in the wrong place at the wrong time. Maybe you've never even had anybody take a swing at you as Mike Leach appeared destined for against SMU.

But perhaps you retaliated when you got one elbow too many in a pickup basketball game. Or maybe you and your spouse or a child into it occasionally, shouting and saying cruel things. Or road rage may be a part of your life.

While we do seem to live in a more belligerent, confrontational society than ever before, fighting is still not the solution to a problem. Rather, it only escalates the whole confrontation, leaving wounded pride, intransigence, and simmering hatred in its wake. Actively seeking and making peace is the way to a solution that lasts and heals broken relationships and aching hearts.

Peacemaking is certainly not as easy as fighting, but it is much more courageous and a lot less painful. It is also exactly what Jesus would do.

If I hadn't been there, I think he might have taken a swing at Mike.
— Bennie Wylie on the '04 SMU game

Making peace instead of fighting takes courage
and strength; it's also what Jesus would do.

DAY 37

PAYBACK

Read Matthew 5:38-42.

"I tell you, Do not resist an evil person. If someone strikes you on the right cheek, turn to him the other also" (v. 39).

Texas Tech may have missed out on a win in its first-ever football game because of an official's desire for revenge.

On Oct. 3, 1925, Tech's first team took the field against the Mc-Murry Indians of McMurry College in Abilene. The game was played at the South Plains Fair Ground because the area "was surrounded by a fence and [it was] easier to keep out non-paying spectators." A good crowd estimated at anywhere between 4,500 to 10,000 turned out for the highlight of fair week.

Despite their inexperience, the Matadors, as the Red Raiders were originally known, dominated the game from the outset. Tech outgained the Indians 222-96 but couldn't get the ball into the end zone, and the game remained scoreless.

Finally, with only a few seconds left on the clock, the Matadors tried a 20-yard field goal. The ball was "hiked" perfectly, and Elson Archibald's drop kick was true. It sailed right between the uprights, and because time had expired on the play, Tech had a 3-0 win in its first-ever game.

Or so it seemed to the jubilant Tech fans who ran onto the field and hoisted Archibald and other players onto their shoulders in celebration. Their joy ended quickly, however, when the umpire ruled that Tech had not gotten the kick off before time had run out. The game was thus a scoreless tie.

Parham C. "Preacher" Callaway was an end in that first-ever game, and he was convinced the Matadors had been swindled. Callaway felt that the official who made the controversial call held a grudge against the new school because he had applied for the head coaching job and had been passed over in favor of E.Y. Freeland. Thus, the ref had made the call out of revenge.

The very nature of the intense rivalries of the Big 12 is that the loser will seek payback for the defeat of the season before. But what about in life when somebody's done you wrong; is it time to get even?

The problem with revenge in real-life is that it isn't as clear-cut as a scoreboard. Life is so messy that any attempt at revenge is often inadequate or, worse, backfires and injures you.

As a result, you remain gripped by resentment and anger, which hurts you and no one else. You poison your own happiness while that other person goes blithely about her business. The only way someone who has hurt you can keep hurting you is if you're a willing participant.

But it doesn't have to be that way. Jesus ushered in a new way of living when he taught that we are not to seek revenge for personal wrongs and injuries. We are to let it go and go on with our lives. What a relief!

[Tech's] first game would create a controversy that would not soon be forgotten by Matador fans and players.
— *Ralph Sellmeyer and James Davidson in* The Red Raiders

Resentment and anger over a wrong injures you, not the other person, so forget it — as Jesus taught.

LAUGH IT UP

Read Genesis 21:1-7.

"Sarah said, 'God has brought me laughter, and everyone who hears about this will laugh with me'" (v. 6).

A Texas Tech press conference once turned humorous when a disgruntled Mike Leach turned the microphones over to a pair of his offensive linemen.

On their way to a sensational 11-win season that ended with a berth in the Cotton Bowl, the 2008 Red Raiders smashed SMU 43-7 in their third game. Despite the easy win, Leach was "steamed about the play of his quarterbacks and receivers in the game." So the head coach tapped senior center Stephen Hamby and junior guard Brandon Carter to speak for the offense at the weekly news conference on Monday.

Hamby got the humor under way when he "offered to push all those receivers who Leach scorned for dropping passes." After all, he had caught a deflected pass in week two's 35-19 defeat of Nevada. "I'm actually trying out for the new 'X' position (Tech's split end)," he told the press. "I heard that was up."

Hamby also told of the SMU game's funniest play. Quarterback Graham Harrell set out to check off the play with 5 seconds left on the play clock. "What are you doing?" Hamby asked, fearing a delay-of-game penalty. So Harrell looked over to All-American receiver Michael Crabtree and shouted for all to hear, "Just run a vertical!" Hamby said he looked up and saw the defense lined up as though they thought Harrell was lying. He wasn't. Touchdown to Crabtree. The center told his quarterback, "Real Mature. Real cool." Harrell's smiling response was, "Did you like that?"

Carter kept the conference lighthearted when he related how he got the black eye he sported. It seems he turned the wrong way during a pregame walk-through at the team hotel and ran into backup center Shawn Byrnes. "I was peeking out half my eye the whole game, but that's all right," Carter said.

Stand-up comedians — even when they're offensive linemen — are successful because they find humor in the world, and it's often hard for us to do that. "Laughter is foolish," an acerbic Solomon wrote in Ecclesiastes 2:2. His angst overwhelmed him because he couldn't find much if anything in his world to laugh at.

We know how he felt. When we take a good look around at this world we live in, can we really find much to laugh at? It seems everywhere we look we find not just godlessness but ongoing and pervasive tragedy and misery.

Well, we can recognize as Sarah did that in God's innumerable gifts lie irresistible laughter. The great gift of Jesus provides us with more than enough reason to laugh no matter our situation. Through God's grace in Jesus Christ, we can laugh at death, at Satan, at the very gates of hell, at the world's pain.

Because they are of this world, our tears will pass. Because it is of God, our laughter will remain — forever.

I just remember the jog to the end zone was tiring.
— Brandon Carter's humorous account of a long TD pass vs. SMU

Of the world, sorrow is temporary;
of God, laughter is forever.

BOSS MAN

Read Matthew 28:16-20.

"Then Jesus came to them and said, 'All authority in heaven and on earth has been given to me'" (v. 18).

At the new head coach's first meeting with his new team, one thing was clear: There was a new boss in town.

Less than 24 hours after he was hired as the head coach of the Texas Tech men's basketball team, legendary college coach Bob Knight met with his seven returning players — at 7 a.m. on Saturday no less. No one complained.

And no one was late. "Oh, no, we were all there bright and early," said junior center Andy Ellis about the meeting on March 24, 2001.

The players showed right away that they had no doubts about who the boss was. "When [Knight] walked into the locker room, it got real quiet," Ellis said.

The announcement of Knight's hiring on Friday, March 23, was the formal acknowledgement of one of the worst-kept secrets in Tech history. Even before he visited Lubbock for an interview, Knight declared he was "livid" over the leaks about his interest in the Tech job. He was hired to resurrect a flagging program that had not been to the NCAA Tournament since 1996.

He took immediate control of Tech men's basketball with that initial team meeting. "He told us the way it's going to be," said junior Jamal Brown. Knight's message was indeed simple and to the point. "He told us three things," Brown reported. "Play hard, play smart and go to class."

Knight effected an immediate turnaround at Tech. His first squad went 23-9 and broke the tournament drought. Over his five-plus years as the Red Raiders' basketball boss, his teams won 138 games, earned four berths in the NCAA Tournament, and failed to win at least 21 games only once.

No matter what our line of work may be, we all have bosses; even if we're self-employed, we work for our customers or clients. One of the key aspects of being an effective boss is spelling out in detail exactly what is expected of those whom the boss directs.

Wouldn't it be helpful if our faith life worked that way, too? Wouldn't it be wonderful if we had a boss who tells us exactly what we are to do? Well, we do.

For Christians, our boss is Jesus, the one to whom all authority on this Earth has been given. As the king of the world, Jesus is the grandest and biggest boss of all. The last thing that boss did before he left us for a while was to deliver a set of instructions. Jesus told us we are to do three things: 1) go and make disciples everywhere; 2) baptize those disciples; and 3) teach those disciples.

There we have it, straight from the head man's mouth just as clear and as precise as we could want it. The real question is how well we are following our boss's instructions.

He let us know that we're going to do things his way and that his way will be a lot different than anything we've ever been through.
— Andy Ellis on the team's first meeting with new boss Bob Knight

The king of the world is our boss,
and he has told us exactly what he wants us to do.

DAY 40

AMAZING!

Read: Luke 4:31-36.

"All the people were amazed and said to each other, 'What is this teaching? With authority and power he gives orders to evil spirits and they come out!'" (v. 36)

Stadium expansions are a routine part of college football. Few — if any — expansions, however, have ever been as amazing as what Texas Tech pulled off in 1959-60.

Several stipulations were part and parcel of Tech's admission into the Southwest Conference in 1956. While the school began competing in all sports in 1957, football had to wait until 1960. The delay was necessary because the league insisted Jones Stadium be expanded to a seating capacity of 40,000.

Several plans for the expansion were considered. Rounding out the north end zone to turn the stadium into a horseshoe was proposed but deemed unsatisfactory because all the additional seating would be in the end zone. Double-decking or building a new stadium off campus was each deemed undesirable.

Eventually, a startling proposal got the green light: move the east stands and excavate between the two sides. That meant pulling off the amazing engineering feat of moving more than six thousand tons of concrete and steel 200 feet.

The firm chosen for the work approached the daunting project as though they were moving a building, or rather seven of them since the stands had originally been built in seven sections. So how did they do it? By rail.

Rollers were placed under three tracks of double sets of rails for each section, and the concrete columns that held up the stands were attached to the rollers. Then, using a single winch truck, the massive structure was inched along. Several men with sledge hammers kept the rollers aligned so the stadium would move in a straight line. The amazing journey took only a few days.

The word *amazing* defines the limits of what you believe to be plausible or usual. The Grand Canyon, the birth of your children, those last-second Tech wins — they're amazing! You've never seen anything like that before!

Some people in Galilee felt the same way when they encountered Jesus. Jesus amazed them with the authority of his teaching, and he wowed them with his power over spirit beings. People everywhere just couldn't quit talking about him.

It would have been amazing had they not been amazed. They were, after all, witnesses to the most amazing spectacle in the history of the world: God himself was right there among them walking, talking, teaching, preaching, and healing.

Their amazement should be a part of your life too because Jesus still lives. The almighty and omnipotent God of the universe seeks to spend time with you every day — because he loves you. Amazing!

The amazing part fascinated 'sidewalk superintendents,' who watched with open mouths.
> — *from* The Red Raiders, *on moving the east stands*

Everything about God is amazing,
but perhaps most amazing of all is that
he loves us and desires our company.

DAY 41

STUBBORN STREAK

Read Ephesians 6:10-20.

"Stand firm then, with the belt of truth buckled around your waist" (v. 14).

Tech offensive coordinator Neal Brown quit being stubborn. The result was a game-clinching drive.

Texas Tech's offensive gurus went into the 2010 season finale against the Houston Cougars on Nov. 27 with a definite plan of attack in mind: They would defeat Houston with the run. "They had struggled against the run, so we came into the game thinking we were going to run the ball," Brown explained.

The ground attack, in fact, netted the touchdown that pushed the Red Raiders into a 27-13 lead early in the third quarter. Quarterback Taylor Potts faked a handoff to senior running back Baron Batch to his left and bootlegged to his right. With the defense chasing Batch, Potts galloped for 28 yards to the Cougar 16. Two plays later, Batch covered the last five yards for the score.

But Houston gambled on fourth down and scored a touchdown with 10 minutes to play that cut Tech's lead to a single score.

That's when Brown decided the time had come to quit being stubborn and give in. All game long Houston had played the run much better than the Tech coaches had expected. "They were moving around up front probably more so than they had done all year," Brown said. Also, he said, "We probably didn't play as well up front running the ball as we had the last few weeks."

So with the outcome of the game still very much in doubt, Brown conceded that it was time to quit being stubborn and turn to the pass. Potts promptly orchestrated an 82-yard touchdown drive in two minutes and 45 seconds. He threw seven times, completing six of them. The last toss was a 19-yard strike to senior receiver Lyle Leong that put the final score of 35-20 on the board.

Stubbornness is not necessarily a virtue as Neal Brown and the Tech offense decided against Houston. Most of us have run across people who are "pigheaded." That is, they won't listen to reason, they won't change their mind, they won't do what everyone else knows they should. They're stubborn for no other reason than that's the way they are.

Sometimes, though, stubbornness can be exactly what a situation demands. We should be stubborn when we know the truth and are called upon to defend it. In no other aspect of our lives is stubbornness more necessary than in our faith.

That's because in Jesus, we know truth. It's not the truth that we vehemently espouse only as long as it is convenient or serves our purposes; that "truth" is what passes for truth in the world. Rather, in Jesus we know absolute truth.

That truth — the soul-saving message of the Gospel — is under attack today, which is nothing new. Just as he always has, Jesus needs stubborn Christians, those who know his truth, live it, and share it with others no matter what "they" say.

I just basically quit being stubborn; probably should have done it earlier.
— Neal Brown on switching to the passing game vs. Houston

To follow Jesus is to be unceasingly
and relentlessly stubborn for him.

DAY 42

QUITE AN IMPRESSION

Read John 1:1-18.

"In the beginning was the Word, and the Word was with God, and the Word was God. . . . The Word became flesh and made his dwelling among us" (vv. 1, 14).

Pete Cawthon made quite an impression on his team at its first day of practice in 1937.

Cawthon was the Tech head football coach from 1930 to 1940. He changed "the image of Texas Tech football, and brought the embryo school national renown in the process."

Cawthon fashioned himself professionally after his friend and idol, the legendary Knute Rockne. The night after Rockne's death in a plane crash in 1931, Cawthon spent the evening sobbing violently. He so hated to lose that on a plane trip home after a loss, he muttered to no one in particular, "I wish this plane would fall and take us all with it." One of his players responded, "Well, he's always tried to live like Rockne. Now he wants to die like him."

Cawthon told his team one day to go home, get their dictionaries, and look up the word "lose." Then, he said, "Cut it out of the dictionary with a razor blade or some scissors. As long as you play for me, there ain't no such word."

On the first day of practice in 1937, Cawthon evidently decided to make an impression on his team, particularly his newcomers. He was not a big man physically, but he told his players in his thick Southern drawl, "I can whip ary man among you." He then singled out quarterback Dempsey Cannon, the smallest man on the team and said, "Is that right, Dempsey?" "That's right, coach," was the reply.

Cawthon then turned to Tor Holcomb, a 265-lb. tackle and the biggest man on the team, repeated the question, and got the same answer. He wheeled to face the whole team and shouted, "There you is from the littlest to the biggest." His impression made, the head coach walked away.

That fetching person in the apartment next door. A job search that comes complete with interview. A class reunion. The new neighbors. We are constantly about the fraught task of wanting to make an impression on people. We want them to remember us, obviously in a flattering way.

We make that impression, good or bad, generally in two ways. Even with instant communication on the Internet — perhaps especially with the Internet — we primarily influence the opinion others have of us by our words. After that, we can advance to the next level by making an impression with our actions.

God gave us an impression of himself in exactly the same way. In Jesus, God took the unprecedented step of appearing to mortals as one of us, as mere flesh and bone. We now know for all time the sorts of things God does and the sorts of things God says. In Jesus, God put his divine foot forward to make a good impression on each one of us.

You know what? I was convinced.
— New Tech player Dudley Aiken after the first day of practice in 1937

Through Jesus' words and actions,
God seeks to impress us with his love.

ULTIMATE MAKEOVER

Read 2 Corinthians 5:11-21.

"If anyone is in Christ, he is a new creation; the old has gone, the new has come!" (v. 17)

When Cody Fuller reported for baseball practice, he was considerably sorer than his teammates. After all, he had just completed a football season.

A wide receiver, Fuller entered Tech on a football scholarship in the fall of 2001. From the moment he stepped on campus, though, he intended to be a two-sport athlete, making himself over into a baseball player in the spring after the football season in the fall.

"It's hard," Fuller admitted about the switch from one sport to another, particularly after seasons like that of 2003-04. He played in the Raiders' 38-14 defeat of Navy in the Houston Bowl of Dec. 30 and then two weeks later showed up for baseball practice. The bumps and bruises of the football season still lingered as he set about quickly changing both his body motions and his mindset to reshape himself into a baseball player. He conceded that playing football didn't really contribute much to his baseball skills. "The only thing that really helps," he said, "is the strength training."

For Fuller, spring football practice took precedence over baseball practice because of the scholarship. He was allowed, however, to miss a practice to play in a baseball game.

Texas Tech baseball head coach Larry Hays was fine with his unusual two-sport player and the compromises it required. "Playing two sports can sometimes be a disadvantage," he said, "but when you get to have the experiences [Fuller] had this year, that might make up for what was missed in baseball."

Fuller didn't just sit around on the bench and claim to be a two-sport athlete. He was a three-year starter in the outfield for Hays; his lowest batting average was .302 as a junior in 2004, and he hit .322 his senior season. For the 8-4 football team of 2004 that beat California in the Holiday Bowl, Fuller caught 43 passes for 505 yards. He was named Tech's Male Student-Athlete of the Year in 2004.

Ever considered a makeover? TV shows show us how changes in clothes, hair, and makeup and some weight loss can radically alter the way a person looks. But these changes are only skin deep. Even with a makeover, the real you — the person inside — remains unchanged. How can you make over that part of you? By giving your heart and soul to Jesus, just as you give up your hair to the stylist or the barber.

You won't look any different; you won't dance any better; you won't suddenly start talking smarter. The change is on the inside where you are brand new because the model for all you think and feel is now Jesus. He is the one you care about pleasing.

Made over by Jesus, you realize that gaining his good opinion — not the world's — is all that really matters. And he isn't the least interested in how you look but how you act.

I think you've got to love this game.
— Cody Fuller on why he played baseball after a tough football season

Jesus is the ultimate makeover artist; he can make you over without changing the way you look.

DAY 44

BELIEVE IT

Read John 3:16-21.

"For God so loved the world that He gave His only begotten Son, that whoever believes in Him should not perish but have everlasting life" (v. 16 NKJV).

I didn't see anybody on our sideline that didn't think we could win." So declared Tech head coach Mike Leach. At the time he was referring to, though, belief in the Red Raiders was probably hard to find away from that sideline.

On Oct. 5, 2002, Tech and Texas A&M played one of the most exciting games in the rivalry's long and storied history. For three quarters, however, the Aggies thrashed Tech soundly. An 82-yard bomb propelled A&M into a 35-17 lead halfway through the third. This was the time Leach spoke about when he said everybody on the sideline still believed. But something had to happen in a hurry. As one writer put it, "At that point, maybe only the players in the Tech huddle sensed something brewing." But it was brewing.

As a shocked, largely maroon-clad crowd looked on in disbelief and horror, the Red Raiders outscored A&M 24-6 in the final 12:22 of the game. Quarterback Kliff Kingsbury pulled Tech close at 35-30 with a pair of touchdown tosses.

Then came the play that almost didn't happen. Wes Welker, the legendary Tech return man, was cramping up so badly on the sideline that special teams coach Manny Matsakis had to ask him if he wanted to go in. Welker believed he could run, and he did —

88 yards worth for a 38-35 Tech lead with 2:48 left.

A&M scored before senior Robert Treece sent the game into overtime with a 42-yard field goal with five seconds left. After an A&M score and a missed extra point, Kingsbury found sophomore wide receiver Nehemiah Glover with a 10-yard touchdown pass. Treece then calmly kicked the PAT for the 48-47 win.

And it happened because the Raiders never stopped believing they could win.

What we believe underscores everything about our lives. Our politics. How we raise our children. How we treat other people. Whether we respect others, their property and their lives.

Often, competing belief systems clamor for our attention; we all know persons — maybe friends and family members — who have lost Christianity in the shuffle, the clamor, and the hubbub. We turn aside from believing in Christ at our peril, however, because the heart and soul, the very essence of Christianity, is belief. That is, believing that this man named Jesus is the very Son of God and through him — and only through him — can we find forgiveness and salvation that will establish for us an eternal home with God.

But believing is more than simply acknowledging intellectually that Jesus is God. Even the demons who serve Satan know that. It is belief so deep that we entrust our lives and our eternity to Christ. We live like we believe it — because we do.

I think everybody believes in this offense.
— Kliff Kingsbury after the '02 A&M game

Believe it: Jesus is the way — and the only way
— to eternal life with God.

BE PREPARED

Read Matthew 10:5-23.

"I am sending you out like sheep among wolves. Therefore be as shrewd as snakes and as innocent as doves" (v. 16).

Tech's preparation for a football game includes, of course, practice and a thorough study of the upcoming opponent. It also includes a comfy bed in a hotel.

During the Mike Leach years, Friday's preparation for a Saturday game always meant packing up and heading to a hotel, even before a home game. The innocuous and longstanding practice became somewhat contentious during the summer of 2009 when officials from the Pac 10 proposed to the NCAA that it be banned to save money. At various times, Leach called the notion "really dumb, "remarkably dumb," and "really a stupid idea."

Under Leach, the Friday routine was inevitably the same. The team gathered for chapel and special-teams work before heading to a hotel. After check-in, the players ate dinner together and then went to a movie. Back at the hotel, they held a team meeting at which Leach and the team captains spoke. The players then split into offense and defense for more meeting before it was lights out.

"I think you have to isolate the main core of the team," Tech defensive coordinator Ruffin McNeill said about the value of the hotel stays. "It keeps us on the same page for a 48-hour period."

The players generally derided the notion that they could be just as prepared for a game by spending the night in their own beds. "You can stay home as much as you want," said senior long snapper Austin Burns. "That doesn't mean you're going to go to bed and get a good night's sleep. A lot of these kids live in apartment complexes where there's parties 'til the sun comes up."

Linebacker Bront Bird declared that if staying in a hotel were banned, the players would respond by bringing their own cots to the Tech facility. At a hotel, he said, "We're able do everything as a team and get our minds ready to play."

Like the Red Raiders, you know the importance of preparation in your own life. You went to the bank for a car loan, facts and figures in hand. That presentation you made at work was seamless because you practiced. Knowing what you need to do and doing what you must to succeed isn't luck; it's preparation.

Jesus understood this, and he prepared his followers by lecturing them and by sending them on field trips. Two thousand years later, the life of faith requires similar training and study. You prepare so you'll be ready when that unsaved neighbor standing beside you at your backyard grill asks about Jesus. You prepare so you will know how God wants you to live. You prepare so you are certain in what you believe when the secular, godless world challenges it.

And one day you'll see God face to face. You certainly want to be prepared for that.

For us, Friday is as big a day as Tuesday [a day of heavy practice].
— Ruffin McNeill on the hotel stays

**Living in faith requires constant study
and training, preparation for the day
when you meet God face to face.**

DAY 46

NOISEMAKER

Read Psalm 100.

"Shout for joy to the Lord, all the earth!" (v. 1)

Tech quarterback Cody Hodges couldn't see what happened, but he didn't need to. He could tell by the crowd noise; it was a massive groan.

On Oct. 8, 2005, the undefeated and 13th-ranked Red Raiders entered Memorial Stadium in Lincoln shooting for their first-ever win there. They got it in one of the most exciting and memorable games in Texas Tech football history.

Tech jumped out to a 21-0 lead in the first half and then saw Nebraska rally to take a 31-27 lead with 5:10 left to play. With a little more than a minute left, Hodges had the offense perched at the Husker 12 — and disaster struck. Hodges' first-down pass was batted into the air, and a Nebraska tackle gathered the ball in for an interception. Game over.

But he headed upfield instead of running out of bounds, and Tech guard Bryan Kegans swatted the ball away. Danny Amendola recovered it, and Tech had life at the Nebraska 19 with 1:13 left.

On fourth down at the Cornhusker 10, Hodges took the snap and was immediately pressured. He first looked left for split end Jarrett Hicks, who was covered. "It's fourth down. I've got to put the ball in play," he later recounted. Scrambling, he spotted wide receiver Joel Filani open at the goal line. "I kind of threw it and let Joel go get it," Hodges said.

With almost 80,000 fans screaming for the Huskers, Hodges went down as the pocket crumbled around him. He thus didn't see whether or not Filani caught the ball since he was on his back looking up at the evening sky. The crowd noise tipped him off, though. It was "the most welcome sound [he] heard all day"; all that ear-shattering noise ceased, replaced by a loud groan.

Filani had indeed caught the ball and scored with 12 seconds left. The Red Raiders had a 34-31 win.

Whether you're at a Tech game live or watching on TV, no doubt you've contributed to the crowd noise generated by thousands of fans or just your buddies. You've probably been known to whoop it up pretty good at some other times in your life, too. The birth of your first child. The concert of your favorite band. That fishing trip when you caught that big ole bass.

But just how many times have you ever let loose with a robust, heartfelt shout to God in response to his love for you? Though God certainly deserves it, he doesn't require that you walk around waving pompoms and shouting "Yay, God!" He isn't particularly interested in having you arrested as a public menace.

No, God doesn't seek a big show or a spectacle. A nice little "thank you" is sufficient when it's delivered from the heart and comes bearing joy. That kind of noise carries all the way to God's home in Heaven; God hears it even if nobody else does.

I was on my back, and I heard 'Ooohhh.' I kind of figured [Joel Filani] caught it and we won the ball game.
— Cody Hodges on the game-winning touchdown he heard

The noise God likes to hear is a heartfelt "thank you," even when it's whispered.

THE OPPORTUNITY

Read Colossians 4:2-6.

"[M]ake the most of every opportunity" (v. 5b).

Wally Dunn finally had the opportunity to shine, and he made the most of it

Dunn was a 6'4" guard who transferred from Midland College and walked on to the Red Raiders basketball team. He played in fourteen games as a sophomore in 2008-09 and in ten games as a junior, scoring 26 points and ten points in the respective seasons. He appeared in fourteen games and scored 15 points his senior season until the Oklahoma game of March 2, 2011.

That was Senior Night, and for the first time Dunn was given the opportunity to start, courtesy of senior David Tairu. Since the squad had six seniors, Tairu yielded his starting spot. "I think it shows how much respect the guys have for Wally," said Raider head coach Pat Knight of Tairu's gesture.

For Dunn, the night was the opportunity of a lifetime, and he didn't waste it. He played so well that the Oklahoma head coach said afterwards he had never seen anything like it from a walk-on on senior night.

One sequence with two minutes to go in the first half demonstrated the intensity Dunn brought to the game. He had an 8-foot jumper blocked. A teammate retrieved the ball and fired it back to Dunn, who put up a three. He missed, got his own rebound, and passed the ball out. Forward Mike Singletary got it to him in the corner, and Dunn shot another trey. Nothing but net.

"You can't have a conscience as a shooter," Dunn deadpanned after the game. "I had no idea I shot three times, to be honest with you, until at halftime."

For the night, the opportunistic Dunn played a season-high 17 minutes in his last home game. He poured in 15 points to help the scarlet and black to an easy 84-58 win over the Sooners.

As was the case with Wally Dunn and his one chance to start and show what he could do, opportunities usually give us only one shot. Miss the chance and it's gone forever. The house you wanted that came on the market; that chance for promotion that opened up, the accidental meeting with that person you've been attracted to from a distance — if the opportunity comes, you have to grab it right now or you may well miss it.

This doesn't hold true in our faith life, however. Salvation through Jesus Christ is not a one-and-done deal. As long as we live, every day and every minute of our life, the opportunity to turn to Jesus is always with us. We have unlimited access to the saving grace of our Lord and Savior.

As with any opportunity, though, we must avail ourselves of it. That is, salvation is ours for the taking but we must take it. The inherent tragedy of an unsaved life thus is not that the opportunity for salvation was withdrawn or was unavailable, but that it was squandered.

You know, it's kind of like the movie Rudy.
— *Pat Knight on Wally Dunn's senior-night game*

We have the opportunity for salvation through Jesus Christ at any time.

DAY 48

MAKE NO MISTAKE

Read Mark 14:66-72.

"Then Peter remembered the word Jesus had spoken to him: 'Before the rooster crows twice you will disown me three times.' And he broke down and wept" (v. 72).

On the final play from scrimmage of what was called "the best game of this college football season," Texas made a mistake.

On Nov. 1, 2008, 7th-ranked and undefeated Texas Tech hosted top-ranked and undefeated Texas, which apparently saved itself with a touchdown and a 33-32 lead with 1:29 left. But as senior Tech quarterback Graham Harrell trotted onto the field after the kickoff, he was smiling. "Game on the line, minute and a half left, you score, you win," he later said. "If you don't love that situation, quarterback's probably not the position for you."

Four straight completions moved the ball to the Texas 28. After an incompletion, the clock had ticked down to 8 seconds. The Tech sideline called "Ace Six," a fancy way of saying everybody go deep. That's when the Longhorns made their fatal mistake.

Among the four Tech receivers who would sprint downfield was Michael Crabtree. The 6'3" All-America was the defending Biletnikoff Award winner as the nation's best receiver; he would win it again. Across the line was a sophomore cornerback making his second start — and he was alone. After the game, Longhorn coaches would insist Crabtree was double covered. Harrell sure didn't see it that way.

Twenty-two yards downfield, Crabtree hit the brakes, turned toward the sideline, and hauled in Harrell's perfectly thrown ball. He then turned upfield rather than going out of bounds. He easily fought off that lone defender's attempt at a tackle and "dug hard for the end zone," crossing the goal line with one second left.

The Raiders had taken advantage of a Longhorn mistake to grab a 39-33 win in one of the biggest games in school history.

It's distressing but it's still true: Like football teams and Simon Peter, we all make mistakes. Only one perfect man ever walked on this earth, and no one of us is he. Some mistakes are just dumb. Like locking yourself out of your car or falling into a swimming pool with your clothes on.

Other mistakes are more significant and carry with them the potential for devastation. Like heading down a path to addiction. Committing a crime. Walking out on a spouse and the children.

All these mistakes, however, from the momentarily annoying to the life-altering tragic, share one aspect: They can all be forgiven in Christ. Other folks may not forgive us; we may not even forgive ourselves. But God will forgive us when we call upon him in Jesus' name.

Thus, the twofold fatal mistake we can make is ignoring the fact that we will die one day and subsequently ignoring the fact that Jesus is the only way to shun Hell and enter Heaven. We absolutely must get this one right.

They tried to man up Crab. [Nobody] can man up Crab.
— Graham Harrell on Texas' single coverage of Michael Crabtree

Only one mistake we make sends us to Hell
when we die: ignoring Jesus while we live.

TEXAS TECH

DAY 49

A SURE THING

Read Romans 8:28-30.

"We know that in all things God works for the good of those who love him, who have been called according to his purpose" (v. 28).

For Spike Dykes, a blue-chip recruit's decision to reject Texas Tech was such a sure thing that he didn't even hear the player tell him he was headed to Lubbock.

Dykes and his staff "fought the living room recruiting wars against Texas and Oklahoma and some of the best programs in the country." One of the most intense battles of the Dykes era was waged over running back Byron Hanspard. "We knew how important he would be to our program," the head coach said.

Rick Dykes, who would eventually serve his father as offensive coordinator, was in charge of recruiting the national blue-chipper. When Hanspard told Rick that he had decided to play for Tech, he asked the coach not to tell anyone of his decision. Rick agreed and didn't even tell his father. A couple of weeks later, father and son had their final visit with Hanspard. The head coach was convinced they were wasting their time.

As Rick told it, his dad was so sure that Hanspard was going somewhere else that when he said he wanted to play for Tech, "my dad responded by telling him he felt he should really keep us in consideration and not rule us out too hastily." Hanspard replied, "Coach, I just told you, I want to go to Tech." When what

Hanspard had said sank in, the head Raider jumped up and distributed high fives all around.

From 1994-96, Hanspard was a sure thing, setting Tech rushing records that still stand (among others) for career yards and most yards in a single game (287 vs. Baylor in '96). He was All-America in 1996 and won the Doak Walker Award as the nation's top running back. He finished sixth in the Heisman Trophy voting.

The outcome of a competitive football game is never a sure thing beforehand. You attend a game expecting the Red Raiders to win, but you don't know for sure. If you did, why bother to go? Any game worth watching carries with it some uncertainty.

Nothing about life is a sure thing either, which means that daily living comes bearing uncertainty. You never know what's going to happen tomorrow or even an hour from now. Oh, sure, you think you know. Right now you may be certain that you'll be at work Monday morning, that you'll have a job next month, and that you'll be happily and comfortably married to the same spouse five years from now. Life's uncertainties, though, can intervene at any time and disrupt those sure things you count on.

Ironically, while you can't know for sure about this afternoon, you can know for certain about forever. Eternity is a sure thing because it's in God's hands. Your unwavering faith and God's sure promises lock in a certain future for you.

Dad was so sure he was going to turn us down, he didn't even hear Byron [Hanspard] say he wanted to come with us.
— *Rick Dykes*

Life is unpredictable and tomorrow is uncertain; only eternity with or without God is a sure thing.

DAY 50

DO WHAT YOU MUST

Read 2 Samuel 12:1-15a.

"The Lord sent Nathan to David" (v. 1).

Tech's head football coach once promised to do whatever it took to keep the program alive, even if he had to coach without pay.

Dell Morgan took over the Raider program in 1941 and led the team to a 9-1 record and a berth in the Sun Bowl. As World War II broke out, many schools set about reluctantly closing up their athletic programs for the duration of the war. Not Morgan. He vowed he would field a football team no matter what it took.

1942 had its challenges. Assistant coach Walker Nichols left before the season ended to begin his stint in the Navy. The Border Conference champion had to be decided by league officials when Hardin-Simmons and Arizona couldn't play because of transportation problems. Their decision cost 4-5-1 Tech the league title.

1943 was more difficult for Morgan. Injuries and active duty left the team with only one letterman, tackle Edward "Buck" Gillenwater. The head coach also had to scratch around to find somebody to play. The season opened against a team from the Lubbock Army Air Field that included Cpl. Rafe "Big Moose" Nabors, a 235-lb. former Tech lineman. Tech won 26-14.

When Gillenwater, end Lee Anderson, and quarterback Freddie Brown reported for active duty, the team was left without any experienced players. Morgan forged ahead by realigning his team. The season included a second game against the Lubbock

Air Field team (a 10-7 loss) and a 14-12 defeat of the South Plains Army Air Field team. Tech finished the season 4-6.

The determined Morgan held his program together even as he continued to lose players in 1944. By the time the season ended with a 7-6 defeat of the South Plains squad, he was putting anybody he could find on the line. The team went 4-7.

When practice started for the '45 season, about eighty players showed up. Morgan had accomplished what he had said he would; he had held the Tech football program together no matter what.

You've had to do some things in your life that you really didn't want to do. Maybe when you put your daughter on severe restriction, broke the news of a death in the family, fired a friend, or underwent surgery. You plowed ahead because you knew it was for the best or you had no choice.

Nathan surely didn't want to confront King David and tell him what a miserable reprobate he'd been, but the prophet had no choice: Obedience to God overrode all other factors. Of all that God asks of us in the living of a godly life, obedience is perhaps the most difficult. After all, our history of disobedience stretches all the way back to the Garden of Eden. The problem is that God expects obedience not only when his wishes match our own but also when they don't.

Obedience to God is a way of life, not a matter of convenience.

The Navy raided our squad and then the Raiders raided us.
    — TCU coach Dutch Meyer after a 40-20 loss to Tech in 1943

**You can never foresee what God will demand
of you, but obedience requires being ready
to do whatever God asks.**

DAY 51

BEYOND THE PAST

Read Colossians 3:1-10.

"You used to walk in these ways, in the life you once lived. But now you must rid yourself of all such things" (vv. 7, 8a).

On their way to yet another season with 20+ wins and a berth in the NCAA Tournament, the Lady Raiders of 2012-13 paused to remember their past.

On Feb. 17, 2013, the Lady Raiders took what was for them a long look into the past, 20 years past. It was a time when the oldest player on the team, senior guard Casey Morris, was all of 3 years old. On the night of a 69-62 defeat of Texas, Texas Tech celebrated the 1993 national champions.

Some may well have questioned the relevance to the 2013 team of something that happened twenty long years ago. The coach was different; Marsha Sharp had moved behind a desk as an assistant athletic director. The arena was different; United Spirit Arena had been the Raiders' home since 1999. Even the conference was different; the league the '93 team played in doesn't exist anymore.

But the Lady Raiders of 2012-13 were battling to get the program back to where it was accustomed to being for so long: winning 20 games or more and playing in the NCAA Tournament. They had missed the Big Dance in 2011-12. The look into the past thus served as a reminder of the "old mojo" that for so many years was part of Texas Tech women's basketball.

"We're just hungry," said senior guard Chynna Brown, who finished up as the team's leading scorer. Tech head coach Kristy Curry felt the look at the 1993 champions helped fuel that hunger to get back on top. "It's important for every team in the country to understand who's come before them and the dues they paid," she said. "It's important to respect the game like that."

Brown said the retrospective gave the whole team a lift as they headed down the season's home stretch. "We watched them play [on tape]," she said. "It was like, 'OK, we need to play that hard.'"

Like the Lady Raiders of 2012-13, we can use the lessons and examples from the past to inspire us and to give us hope. All too often, though, in our lives we allow our own past to haunt us like a persistent, annoying ghost. We lug our regrets around along with memories of our past failures, omissions, and shortcomings, donning them each day like old clothes.

Short of utter callousness and severe memory problems, only one way exists to free ourselves totally from the past: the change offered through salvation in Jesus Christ. Even when we fall on our knees in despair and cry out to Jesus, we sometimes falsely believe that salvation and forgiveness can never be ours. That's because many desperate seekers fall prey to the fallacy that they must be perfect before Jesus will accept them. The truth is that we need Jesus because we are not perfect.

Jesus didn't die for our past but for our future. He died to free us from the past and to replace it with a glorious future.

I think you embrace the past; you don't run from it or ignore it.
— Lady Raiders head coach Kristy Curry

Every saint has a past; every sinner has a future.

DAY 52

BLACK MAGIC

Read Isaiah 2:6-16.

"They are full of superstitions from the East; . . . they bow down to the work of their hands" (vv. 6b, 8b).

Texas Tech beat Texas A&M so resoundingly that an Aggie lineman could only attribute the defeat to "some type of black magic."

Year after year, the Red Raiders and the Aggies put on some of the most riveting games in Big 12 conference history. The series became known for its "singularly memorable plays and fantastic finishes." Such a game was generally expected on Oct. 4, 2003. After all, for nine years in a row the match-up had been decided by a touchdown or less or was that close in the fourth quarter. This time it didn't happen.

Tech unleashed senior quarterback B.J. Symons on the helpless Aggies, jumped out to an early lead, and never looked back. When the clock mercifully ticked down to zero to end the game, Tech had waxed A&M 59-28. It was the most thorough whipping the Raiders had administered to the Aggies since a 41-9 romp in 1954 when Bear Bryant was the head coach at College Station.

Tech had no trouble moving the ball early, jumping out to a quick 17-0 lead by the end of the first quarter. In the third quarter, just when the Aggies showed a little life, the home team spurted to 21 quick points.

The A&M defense could do nothing with Symons, who set a conference record by throwing eight touchdown passes. Three scoring tosses went to Nehemiah Glover, two to Wes Welker. He finished with 505 yards on 34-of-46 passing. The 59 points was the most given up by A&M in school history.

In a futile attempt to find some reason for the debacle, Aggie offensive lineman Alan Reuber could only resort to superstition. He said after the game, "There must be some type of black magic out here, and I just can't explain it."

Superstitions — such as Alan Reuber's attributing A&M's loss to a nebulous "black magic" — can be quite benign. Nothing in the Bible warns us about the dangers inherent in walking under ladders or spilling table salt.

God is quite concerned, however, about superstition of a more serious nature such as using the occult to predict the future. Its danger for us is that we allow something other than God to take precedence in our lives; we, in effect, worship idols.

While most of us scoff at palm readers and psychics, we nevertheless risk being idol worshippers of a different sort. Just watch the frenzied reaction of fans when a movie star or a star football player shows up. Or consider how we often compromise what we know is right merely to save face or to gain favor in the workplace.

Superstition is the stuff of nonsense. Idol worshipping, however, is as real for us today as it was for the Israelites. It is also just as dangerous.

It's a weird deal.
— Aggie lineman Alan Reuber on the 59-28 loss to Tech

Superstition in the form of idol worship is alive and well today, occurring anytime we venerate anything other than God.

THE SYMBOL

Read Mark 15:16-32.

"Let this Christ, this king of Israel, come down now from the cross, that we may see and believe" (v. 32a).

As he prepared his team for a bowl game, Tech's head coach decided the school and his team needed a symbol, so he came up with one. As it turned out, he had a very good idea.

DeWitt Weaver's Red Raiders of 1953 set a school record with 11 wins, (subsequently tied by Jim Carlen's 1973 squad and Mike Leach's 2008 team). The successful season landed the team in the Gator Bowl against Auburn on Jan. 1, 1954.

DeWitt had observed that unlike other schools, Tech had no visible and recognizable symbol for its team. He called a junior animal husbandry major, Joe Kirk Fulton, into his office and told him, "I've got an idea maybe you and I can work out." That idea was the Masked Rider.

An expert horseman, Fulton quickly agreed to the plan and went to work. He first borrowed a horse named Blackie from a member of the Levelland Sheriff's Posse; then he assembled his costume of jeans, a red shirt, a red and black cape, and a black hat. The horse was taken to Jacksonville by train for the Gator Bowl.

The first-ever Masked Rider then led the team onto the Gator Bowl turf — and was met by stunned disbelief and silence. That lasted only momentarily, though, before Red Raider fans burst into applause. Ed Danforth of the *Atlanta Journal* wrote, "No team in any bowl game ever made a more sensational entrance."

The Red Raiders have been making sensational entrances ever since. Today, to be chosen as the Masked Rider is one of the highest honors a student can achieve. The selection comes only after an arduous and challenging application process.

After all, "the Masked Rider is uniquely Texas Tech."

Symbols are powerful factors in our lives. Consider the wellspring of emotions, thoughts, and sensations the passing by of the American flag elicits in many of us. Witness, too, the power of the Masked Rider to generate unbounded enthusiasm and joy when he leads the Red Raiders onto the field.

Some symbols — such as company logos like the swoosh and the golden arches — are carefully chosen. Others seem to arrive as if by accident or through custom. Christianity's most recognized and beloved symbol is one of the latter. It is the cross, perhaps the most unlikely choice for a symbol in history.

After all, in its time, the cross was a symbol for the ultimate ignominy, the means of execution for the Roman Empire's most scorned criminals and lowlifes. And our lord died on one of them.

Yet, today, for Christians to boldly and openly proclaim their faith for everyone to see, they need only wear a cross. What once symbolized death and despair has become a symbol of hope and love. Such is the transforming power of God through Jesus.

[The Masked Rider] represents one of the most noble and glamorous traditions alive today — not only at Texas Tech, but at any university.
— Texas Tech Center for Campus Life Spirit Program

**As it did with the cross, God's love can take
our ugly lives and make them beautiful.**

DAY 54

BAD IDEA

Read Mark 14:43-50.

"The betrayer had arranged a signal with them: 'The one I kiss is the man; arrest him and lead him away under guard'" (v. 44).

During the process that led to Mike Leach's taking the head coaching job at Tech, everyone involved had one really bad idea.

The offensive coordinator at Oklahoma, Leach interviewed for the Red Raider job three times in 1999. The first session took place at a hotel in Oklahoma City late in the season and was rather routine. The Tech brass decided they wanted a second interview, which turned into a complete disaster because of what seemed like a pretty good idea at the time. At the first interview, the collective decision was made to hold the second interview in Lubbock after the Tech-Oklahoma game of Nov. 20.

"I didn't have much experience interviewing for a head coaching job and couldn't see all the pitfalls lying in wait," Leach later said. He quickly learned.

The media soon discovered Leach's plans to hang around after the game and interview for the Tech job. What those involved had expected was another quiet, purposeful session that would move the process forward. What they got was a circus.

The result, Leach recalled, was "a total distraction for the OU team, which wasn't fair to our players. I didn't foresee that and [OU head coach] Bob [Stoops] didn't either." When the Sooners arrived in Lubbock, the town was abuzz with talk about Leach's taking over the Tech program. The consensus was that the interview after the game would rubber-stamp Leach's hiring.

"We ended up playing poorly," Leach said. In Spike Dykes' last game, freshman quarterback Kliff Kingsbury made his first start and led the Raiders to a 38-28 upset.

The bad idea that resulted in a major distraction for the Sooners turned out to be a very good idea for the Tech football team.

That sure-fire investment you made from a pal's hot stock tip. The expensive exercise machine that now traps dust bunnies under your bed. Blond hair. Telling your wife you wanted to eat at the restaurant with the waitresses in the skimpy shorts. They seemed like pretty good ideas at the time; they weren't.

We all have bad ideas in our lifetime. They provide some of our most crucial learning experiences. Mike Leach, for instance, learned a great deal about job interviews from the ruckus of 1999.

Some ideas, though, are so irreparably and inherently bad that we cannot help but wonder why they were even conceived in the first place. Almost two thousand years ago a man had just such an idea. Judas' betrayal of Jesus remains to this day one of the most heinous acts of treachery in history.

Turning his back on Jesus was a bad idea for Judas then; it's a bad idea for us now.

The idea was, we go to Lubbock to play Tech, and then after the game I'd stick around and have my second interview. Bad idea.
— Mike Leach

We all have some bad ideas in our lives; nothing equals the folly of turning away from Jesus.

DAY 55

CALLING IT QUITS

Read Numbers 13:25-14:4.

"The men who had gone up with him said, 'We can't attack those people; they are stronger than we are'" (v. 13:31).

Not even a cancer diagnosis in the middle of the season could make Patience Knight quit.

Knight is the greatest shot put thrower in Texas Tech women's track and field history, holding the school records for both indoor and outdoor throws. She was a sophomore in February 2007 when she was diagnosed with cancer after a fist-sized tumor was discovered near her heart.

Her coach, Wes Kittley, at once turned his thoughts away from competition to concerns about saving Knight's life. To his surprise, she told him that not only was she not quitting for the season but she wasn't going to stop training and would compete. The doctors had told her that keeping the same routine would help her body fight off the cancer. "I couldn't believe it," Kittley said.

Some days, Knight came to workouts directly after undergoing chemotherapy. Thus, she battled energy and weight loss and nausea even as she trained. "It was hard at first," she admitted, "but then I just stopped feeling sorry for myself. I just never lost faith in God or in my abilities." As the season progressed she got stronger, eventually qualifying for the NCAA championships.

During one competition that season, Knight mentioned that

she wasn't feeling "quite right." When she returned home, doctors discovered that a portion of the catheter used to administer her chemo had broken off and fallen into her heart. The damage was repaired surgically, and Knight went back to work.

Never quitting, Knight went on to be a two-time All-America. As a senior in 2009, she won both the indoor and outdoor Big 12 titles. In 2008, she won the Honda Inspiration Award, presented to an outstanding female college athlete who has overcome adversity to excel in her sport.

Remember that time you quit a high-school sports team? That night you bailed out of a relationship? Walked away from a job with the goals unachieved? Sometimes quitting is the most sensible way to minimize your losses, so you may well at times in your life give up on something or someone.

In your relationship with God, however, you should remember the people of Israel, who quit when the Promised Land was theirs for the taking. They forgot one fact of life you never should: God never gives up on you.

That means you should never, ever give up on God. No matter how tired or discouraged you get, no matter that it seems your prayers aren't getting through to God, no matter what — quitting on God is not an option.

He is preparing a blessing for you, and in his time, he will bring it to fruition — if you don't quit on him.

In Patience [Knight], we have the example of someone who won't quit.
— Tech track and field coach Wes Kittley

Whatever else you give up on in your life, don't give up on God; he will never ever give up on you.

PARTY ANIMALS

Read Exodus 14:26-31; 15:19-21.

"Miriam the prophetess, Aaron's sister, took a tambourine in her hand, and all the women followed her, with tambourines and dancing" (v. 15:20).

It was party time in Lubbock!

"That was the first [time] I've ever been around something like that." For Texas Tech defensive tackle Ra'Jon Henley, the "something like that" was the party Red Raider fans threw on Nov. 17, 2007, after the team's upset of third-ranked Oklahoma.

A season that had started at 6-1 had run into trouble when the Raiders lost three of four to fall to 7-4. It didn't promise to get a whole lot better when Oklahoma came to town. The 9-1 Sooners had a clear shot at the national title after the team ranked No. 2 lost on Thursday night. All they had to do was win.

They didn't, though they certainly started out like they would romp. Just five plays into the game, OU intercepted a pass and took it the distance. 7-zip. But the resilient Tech team shook off the setback. After a pair of field goals from Alex Trlica, Graham Harrell sneaked in from the 1 for a 13-7 Tech lead.

Oklahoma never recovered. The Raider defense held OU to 112 yards in the first half, and the home team blew out to a 27-10 lead. The Sooners rallied in the fourth quarter but couldn't save themselves. Tech won 34-27.

And the party began. Thousands of fans, many of them students, stormed the field. Harrell found himself getting a free ride atop the shoulders of some of them.

Henley, who had never seen such a reaction before, was unsure at first what to make of all the commotion. As he watched the mob flood the field, he said he "didn't know if they were going to jump on me or what. I was just trying to get to my parents. They were all saying, 'Great game,' stuff like that."

They were throwing a party, and he was among the guests of honor.

You know what it takes to throw a good party. You start with your closest friends, add some salsa and chips, fire up the grill and throw on some burgers and dogs, and then top it all off with the Tech game on TV.

You probably also know that just about any old excuse will do to get some people together for a celebration. All you really need is a sense that life is pretty good right now.

That's the thing about having Jesus as part of your life: He turns every day into a celebration of the good life. No matter what tragedies or setbacks life may have in store — and they will come — the heart given to Jesus will find the joy in living. That's because such a life is spent with quiet confidence in God's promise of salvation through Jesus, a confidence that inevitably bubbles up into a joy the troubles of the world cannot touch.

When a life is celebrated with Jesus, the party never stops.

It was great. I didn't want to leave the field.
    — Tech safety Joe Garcia on the party after the win over OU

**With Jesus, life is one big party,
a celebration of victory and joy.**

DAY 57

UNBELIEVABLE!

Read Hebrews 3:7-19.

"See to it, brothers, that none of you has a sinful, unbelieving heart that turns away from the living God" (v. 12).

The Red Raiders were done, kaput. They had blown a big lead in the fourth quarter, and Fresno State had the ball with the last minute ticking away. Then something unbelievable happened.

The Raiders were looking to start the season at 3-0 when they hosted the Bulldogs on Sept. 19, 1998. They withstood a fourth-quarter Fresno rally and were in pretty good shape with a 27-22 lead and the ball as the fourth quarter wound down.

Then the game turned unbelievable.

With 4:04 left, Fresno intercepted a pass and took it back all the way to lead 28-27. Tech didn't even need a play from scrimmage to apparently take over the game again. Sophomore John Norman gathered in the kickoff 3 yards deep in the end zone and took it out. He sprinted 86 yards before he was tackled at the Bulldog 14. Even if Tech didn't get a touchdown, a field goal was a sure thing.

Maybe not. The Raiders moved to a second-and-goal at the 6 when the unbelievable happened: They fumbled right at the goal line and Fresno State recovered. The Dogs hunkered down at the 1 as the clock ticked away the last minute. Game over.

But then came the most unbelievable play of all in the game's furious finish. The Bulldogs did what they had to, running safe plays straight ahead to gain a little room for a punt and to make Tech use its time outs. On third down, Reagan Bownds, a junior linebacker and a former walk-on, hit the State back, who had not fumbled a single time the season before, and the ball popped free. It landed right in the welcoming arms of middle linebacker Kyle Shipley. With 48 seconds left, he stepped off the one yard that was all he needed for a touchdown.

Unbelievably, Texas Tech had a 34-28 win.

Much of what taxes the limits of our belief system has little effect on our lives. Maybe we don't believe in UFOs, honest politicians, aluminum baseball bats, Sasquatch, or the viability of electric cars. A healthy dose of skepticism is a natural defense mechanism that helps protect us in a world that all too often has designs on taking advantage of us.

That's not the case, however, when Jesus and God are part of the mix. Quite unbelievably, we often hear people blithely assert they don't believe in God. Or brazenly declare they believe in God but don't believe Jesus was anything but a good man and a great teacher.

At this point, unbelief becomes dangerous because God doesn't fool around with scoffers. He locks them out of the Promised Land, which isn't a country in the Middle East but Heaven itself.

Given that scenario, it's downright unbelievable that anyone would not believe.

Sometimes it's better to be lucky than good.
— *Kyle Shipley on the unbelievable finish to the '98 Fresno State game*

Perhaps nothing is as unbelievable as that some people insist on not believing in God or his son.

IN THE KNOW

Read John 4:19-26, 39-42.

"They said to the woman, . . . 'Now we have heard for ourselves, and we know that this man really is the Savior of the world'" (v. 42).

Larry Hays just knew. It was time to go.

As June 2008 began, Texas Tech's veteran head baseball coach was in Decatur, Ala., watching his son, Shanon, coach his softball team to the NAIA national title. He was having trouble concentrating on the game, though, because he kept talking to himself and thinking about Tech baseball.

For 22 wonderful years, Hays had led the Red Raider program. Well, maybe the first few years weren't so wonderful. Hays took over the Tech baseball team in 1987, and the program had a long history of ineptness in the Southwest Conference. "For years, and this may sound bad," Hays said, "the Southwest Conference used Texas Tech. . . . In a sense, we felt abused." In other words, Tech was a punching bag for other, more successful programs.

Hays changed all that. He said that by the early 1990s, "When we [went] places, we [were] considered one of the top teams in the country." During one season in the mid 1990s, the Red Raiders were ranked No. 2 in the nation as they batted and pitched their way to the NCAA tournament.

Hays sat that day in Decatur and reviewed his career. His teams had made nine NCAA tournament appearances. His '95 squad had set a school record with 51 wins. He had overseen the move to the Big 12 Conference without a hitch; the Raiders went 23-7 in league play in their first season in the new neighborhood. He had started the day fully intending to coach at least one more season.

So what was the problem that had Hays carrying on a conversation with himself? Something about staying on didn't feel right. As he sat there, he just knew something in the same way that he knew when to put the bunt on in a game. It was time to retire. Monday morning in Lubbock, Hays handed in his resignation.

Larry Hays just knew in the same way that you know certain things in your life. That your spouse loves you, for instance. That you are good at your job. That tea should be iced and sweetened. That a bad day fishing is still better than a good day at work. You know these things even though no mathematician or philosopher can prove any of this on paper.

It's the same way with faith in Jesus: You just know that he is God's son and the savior of the world. You know it in the same way that you know the Red Raiders are the only team worth pulling for: with every fiber of your being, with all your heart, your mind, and your soul. You know it despite the mindless babble and blasphemy of the unbelievers.

You just know, and because you know him, Jesus knows you. And that is all you really need to know.

I always asked (friends) how will I know, what is the sign? (One) way is you just know.
— *Larry Hays on stepping down*

**A life of faith is lived in certainty and conviction:
You just know you know.**

AS A RULE

Read Luke 5:27-32.

"Why do you eat and drink with tax collectors and 'sinners'?" (v. 30b)

In Tech's second football season, an alert player took advantage of the rules to score a touchdown that gained the team a win.

Before the 1926 season started, the 25 players who made up the first-ever Texas Tech football team of the previous season were presented with blankets in honor of their surprising 6-1-2 record. Team captain Hurley Carpenter, a tackle, delivered an acceptance speech on behalf of the team at a convocation of the student body.

The '26 season featured the first home games played on campus and the first-ever encounter with a Southwest Conference team. Enthusiasm was so high that private donors ponied up the money for the band to make the trip to Fort Worth for the TCU game.

The second season saw a couple of strange games. The contest against Schreiner Institute from Kerrville was played on a rain-soaked field and ended in a scoreless tie. With neither team able to generate any offense in the mud, the squads combined to punt an astounding 44 times. Texas Tech could manage only three first downs while Schreiner didn't have a single one.

The season opener against McMurry College featured a touchdown that would not be possible under today's rules. In the fourth quarter, the Indians punted, and a coverage man downed the ball on the Tech 42. Elson Archibald, who the season before had kicked a field goal to score the first points in Tech gridiron history, nonchalantly walked over, picked up the ball, and took off. While the other 21 players stood around and watched, he went 58 yards for what was ruled a touchdown because the ball had never been blown dead as it would have been under today's rules. Archibald then kicked the extra point for the 7-0 win.

As college football players do, you live by rules that others set up. Some lender determined the interest rate on your mortgage and your car loan. You work hours and shifts somebody else established. Someone else decided what day your garbage gets picked up and what school district your house is in.

Jesus encountered societal rules also, including a strict set of religious edicts that dictated what company he should keep, what people, in other words, were fit for him to socialize with, talk to, or share a meal with. Jesus ignored the rules, choosing love instead of mindless obedience and demonstrating his disdain for society's rules by mingling with the outcasts, the lowlifes, the poor, and the misfits.

You, too, have to choose when you find yourself in the presence of someone whom society deems undesirable. Will you choose the rules or love? Are you willing to be a rebel for love — as Jesus was for you?

I believe in rules. Sure I do. If there weren't any rules, how could you break them?
— *Baseball hall of famer Leo Durocher*

**Society's rules dictate who is acceptable
and who is not, but love in the name of Jesus
knows no such distinctions.**

DAY 60

HURRY UP AND WAIT

Read Acts 1:1-14.

"Do not leave Jerusalem, but wait for the gift my Father promised, which you have heard me speak about" (v. 4).

For five years, Seth Doege waited to play quarterback for Texas Tech. In the end, it was all worth the wait.

When Doege committed to Texas Tech as a high-school junior in the fall of 2006, he was ready to live out his childhood dream. Before his season started, though, he tore his left ACL and missed his junior year rehabbing his injury. Then he tore his right ACL in pre-season practice and missed his senior season as well.

After each injury, a disappointed Doege, concerned that Tech would withdraw its offer, called the coaching staff. Each time the coaches reassured him that he was their guy.

After two years of waiting on the sideline, Doege arrived in Lubbock in the fall of 2008 to find that his wait was really only beginning. He was redshirted, started one game in 2009 when Taylor Potts and backup Steve Sheffield were both injured, and then threw only four passes as a sophomore in 2010.

Finally, in 2011, after five years, Doege's wait was over; he was Tech's starting quarterback. In his second start, he completed 40 of 44 passes in a 59-13 defeat of New Mexico, setting a major college record for the highest completion percentage. The record had been held by former Tech quarterback Kliff Kingsbury. When Doege threw for 441 yards and four touchdowns in the 41-38 upset of third-ranked Oklahoma in Norman on Nov. 13, he was named the National Player of the Week.

Doege ended his two seasons as a starter third in Tech history in passing yards, touchdowns, and completions at the time. Graham Harrell (2006-08) and he are the only two Tech quarterbacks to throw for more than 4,000 yards in consecutive seasons.

For Seth Doege and for Tech fans, the wait was worth it.

You rush to your doctor's appointment and wind up sitting in the appropriately named waiting room for an hour. You wait in the concessions line at a Texas Tech game. You're put on hold when you call a tragically misnamed "customer service" center. All of that waiting is time in which we seem to do nothing but feel the precious minutes of our life ticking away.

Sometimes we even wait for God. We have needs, and we desperately call upon the Lord and are disappointed when we perhaps get no immediate answer.

But Jesus' last command to his disciples was to wait. Moreover, the entire of our Christian life is spent in an attitude of waiting for Jesus' return. While we wait for God, we hold steadfast to his promises, we continue our ministry, we remain in communion with him through prayer and devotion.

In other words, we don't just wait; we grow stronger in our faith. Waiting for God is never time lost.

We knew that it was going to take some time.
— Seth Doege's dad on his son's long wait to start at Texas Tech

Since God acts on his time and not ours,
we often must wait for him,
using the time to strengthen our faith.

DAY 61

ROCK SOLID

Read Luke 6:46-49.

"I will show you what he is like who comes to me and hears my words and puts them into practice. He is like a man building a house, who dug down deep and laid the foundation on rock" (vv. 47-48).

Tech was already in the Southwest Conference when JT King took over the football program. He laid the foundation that ensured they belonged there and, eventually, in the Big 12.

The Red Raiders had just one win and one tie to show for their rookie season in the Southwest Conference, which was 1960. De-Witt Weaver, the coach and athletic director who was primarily responsible for securing that long-held dream of membership in the SWC, resigned. King, Weaver's first assistant, was promoted.

He did not step into a good situation. Tech's athletic facilities "were grossly inadequate." The program was so broke that "long distance calls had to be cleared through administrative offices." The football team "was devoid of talent even by Border Conference standards," the Raiders' home before the SWC.

King set about laying a foundation that would make the Red Raiders perennial contenders. The team improved to 5-5 in 1963, 6-4-1 and a Sun Bowl berth in '64, and the 8-3 Gator Bowl season of 1965 with a second-place finish in the conference.

King always said that the program's breakthrough win was the 19-13 defeat of Texas in Austin in 1967. Quarterback John Scovell ran for one TD and tossed another. All-American kicker Kenny Vinyard provided the margin of victory with a pair of field goals.

So many fans met the team plane that it couldn't land at the Lubbock airport. The pilot had to fly to Amarillo and wait for the crowd to disperse.

The foundation had been laid; the Red Raiders belonged.

You can't build anything solid and lasting unless there's a good foundation. That goes for college athletics programs and for your life, both works in progress. As with any complex construction job, if your life is to be stable, it must have a solid foundation, which holds everything up and keeps everything together.

R. Alan Culpepper said in *The New Interpreter's Bible*, "We do not choose whether we will face severe storms in life; we only get to choose the foundation on which we will stand." In other words, tough times are inevitable. If your foundation isn't rock-solid, you will have nothing on which to stand as those storms buffet you, nothing to keep your life from flying apart into a cycle of disappointment and destruction.

But when the foundation is solid and sure, you can take the blows, stand strong, recover, and live with joy and hope. Only one foundation is sure and foolproof: Jesus Christ. Everything else you build upon will fail you.

He is the man who laid the mortar for a solid SWC foundation for Texas Tech.
— The Red Raiders *on JT King*

In the building of your life, you must start with a foundation in Jesus Christ, or the first trouble that shows up will knock you down.

DAY 62

A SECOND CHANCE

Read John 7:53-8:11.

"'Then neither do I condemn you,' Jesus declared. 'Go now and leave your life of sin'" (v. 8:11).

Jamal Brown got a second chance — and the Red Raiders had a basketball upset of Oklahoma.

On Jan. 16, 2001, Tech battled the 22nd-ranked Sooners right down to the wire. In fact, the Red Raiders appeared to be cruising when they took a 50-42 lead with 11:14 to play. Oklahoma rallied, though, and pulled to within 58-57 as the clock ticked down to under a minute.

That's when Brown took a shot he probably would have liked to have back. A guard, Brown was the third leading scorer on the team behind center Andy Ellis and forward Cliff Owens. With 45 seconds left on the clock — but more importantly with 15 seconds still on the shot clock — Brown launched a 3 from the right wing. He missed and OU got the rebound with lots of time left.

"I thought about whether I should have taken that after I missed it," Brown said after the game. "You don't really want to take the shot that early in the shot clock." But he did.

Oklahoma scored on a drive through the lane to take a 59-58 lead with 28.4 seconds on the clock. Tech head coach James Dickey called a timeout to set up the play, calling for two different ones depending on the defense OU employed.

Brown calmly brought the ball down the court amid yells from a smattering of OU fans to "jack up another shot like the one before!" This time Brown stayed outside the arc until the clock ticked down to 8 seconds. Then he moved inside, and when no one moved over to double on him, he drove to the hoop. He put up a soft, spinning 5-foot bank shot that bounced once and went in with 1.5 seconds left.

He couldn't see it, so he didn't know the ball had gone in until the crowd let loose with a massive roar. Jamal Brown had made good on his second chance, and Tech had a 60-59 win.

"If I just had a second chance, I know I could make it work out." Ever said that? If only you could go back and tell your dad one last time you love him, take that job you passed up rather than relocate, or replace those angry shouts at your son with gentle encouragement. If only you had a second chance, a mulligan.

As the story of Jesus' encounter with the adulterous woman illustrates, with God you always get a second chance. No matter how many mistakes you make, God will never give up on you. Nothing you can do puts you beyond God's saving power. You always have a second chance because with God your future is not determined by your past or who you used to be. It is determined by your relationship with God through Jesus Christ.

God is ready and willing to give you a second chance — or as many chances as it takes — if you will give him a chance.

I looked up at the clock and saw just a second remaining and said to myself, (Oklahoma) is just going to need a prayer.
— *Jamal Brown on his second chance*

**You get a second chance with God
if you give him a chance.**

CHEAP TRICKS

Read Acts 19:11-20.

"The evil spirit answered them, 'Jesus I know, and I know about Paul, but who are you?'" (v. 15)

Wes Welker did it all against Texas. He even called the trick play that clinched the win.

The Tech legend had a game for the ages against the Texas Longhorns on Nov. 16, 2002. He hauled in a school-record 14 passes, ran the ball four times, returned three punts, scored two touchdowns, recorded one tackle, and even downed a punt. After the game, Tech head coach Mike Leach pointed out the one thing Welker hadn't done. "The word is the one Achilles heel [Welker] might have is that I don't know that he throws the ball very good," Leach joked.

In addition to all that physical activity, Welker made one of the game's biggest plays with his head, not with his hands. He called the trick play that clinched the 42-38 win over the 4th-ranked Longhorns.

With less than three minutes to play, the Raiders drew a false-start penalty on third down as they tried to run out the clock. That left them facing third and 9 from their own 36. The situation was quite clear. A conversion would ice the game. Failure to convert the first down would mean a punt. Texas would get the ball back with enough time to win it.

On the sideline, the Tech brain trust discussed its options when

Welker leaned over to Leach. He told him to call a trick play. He wanted quarterback Kliff Kingsbury to throw a lateral to receiver Mickey Peters, who would then sail it downfield — to none other than Welker. "It was just a feeling," Welker said about the call. "It was something they didn't expect to happen."

The Horns didn't expect it at all because they blitzed a safety. Welker was wide open and hauled in Peters' pass for a 35-yard gain and a first down. Game over.

Scam artists are everywhere — and they love trick plays. An e-mail encourages you to send money to some foreign country to get rich. That guy at your front door offers to resurface your driveway at a ridiculously low price. A TV ad promises a pill to help you lose weight without diet or exercise.

You've been around; you check things out before deciding. The same approach is necessary with spiritual matters, too, because false religions and bogus Christian denominations abound. The key is what any group does with Jesus. Is he the son of God, the ruler of the universe, and the only way to salvation? If not, then what the group espouses is something other than the true Word of God.

The good news about Jesus does indeed sound too good to be true, but the only catch is that there is no catch. When it comes to salvation through Jesus Christ, there's no trick lurking in the fine print. There's just the truth, right there for you to see.

Welker made the suggestion. He likes to get the ball a lot.
— *Kliff Kingsbury on Wes Welker's trick-play call vs. Texas*

God's promises through Jesus sound too good to be true, but the only catch is that there is no catch.

DAY 64

THE PANIC BUTTON

Read Mark 4:35-41.

"He said to his disciples, 'Why are you so afraid? Do you still have no faith?'" (v. 40)

Panic perhaps should have prevailed in the Tech locker room at halftime of the 2008 A&M game. Instead, calm reigned, and the Raiders came out the last half and blew the Aggies away.

The undefeated (6-0) Red Raiders were favored by three touchdowns over the 2-4 Aggies on Oct. 18 in College Station. Instead of being a willing victim, the A&M offense "sliced and diced" its way through the Tech defense to a 23-20 halftime lead. Seemingly moving at will, the Aggies scored five times on six possessions. The Red Raider offense contributed to the debacle with a pair of turnovers that led to ten Aggie points.

So with one of the greatest seasons in school history on the line and with a "typically raucous and swaying" Kyle Field crowd doing its best to disrupt them, the Raiders could well have felt the clutch of panic about their throats. Led by a calm Mike Leach, however, there was none of that. "It was more of a relaxation session than anything," the head coach said about what went on in the locker room at the break. "No fire and brimstone this time."

Leach calmly preached patience to his team. "Everybody just settled down," running back Baron Batch said about halftime. "Coach Leach said, 'Play like you practice on Wednesday and we'll get the win.' That's what we did, and that's what happened."

Indeed. The result of all that calm and patience was a complete turnaround. The defense pitched a shutout the last half, giving up only four first downs and 32 total yards. In the fourth quarter, the offense put together two time-consuming, back-breaking drives. The first went 80 yards in 13 plays, the second 76 yards in 12 plays.

When it all ended, the panic-free Raiders had a 43-25 win.

Have you ever experienced that suffocating sensation of fear as it escalates into full-blown panic? Maybe the time when you couldn't find your child at the mall or at the beach? Or the heart-stopping moment when you realized that vehicle speeding right toward you wasn't going to be able to stop?

As the story of the disciples and the storm illustrates, the problem with panic is that it debilitates us. While some of them were landlubbers unaccustomed to bad weather in a boat, the storm panicked even the professional fishermen among them into help-lessness. All they could do was wake up an exhausted Jesus.

We shouldn't be too hard on them, though, because we often make an even more grievous mistake. They panicked and turned to Jesus; we panic and often turn away from Jesus by underesti-mating both his power and his ability to handle our crises.

We have a choice when fear clutches us. We can assume Jesus no longer cares for us, surrender to it, and descend into panic. Or we can remember how much Jesus loves us and resist fear and panic by trusting in him.

I was proud of them for that.
— Mike Leach on the lack of panic in the Tech halftime locker room

To plunge into panic is to believe that Jesus is incapable of handling the crises in our lives.

STRANGE BUT TRUE

Read Philippians 2:1-11.

"And being found in appearance as a man, he humbled himself and became obedient to death — even death on a cross!" (v. 7)

It's strange but true: The Texas Tech football team once played two games in one weekend.

After playing as an independent since the football program's inception in 1925, the Matadors joined the Border Conference prior to the 1932 season. Founded in 1931, the league's charter members were the current schools of Arizona, Arizona State, Northern Arizona, New Mexico, and New Mexico State. Tech remained in the league through 1956; it disbanded in 1962.

Tech's admission to the league came on such short notice that only two conference teams could be scheduled for the 1932 season. The first of these — against Arizona — was set for a weekend when Tech already had a game scheduled against New Mexico Normal. Head coach Pete Cawthon decided against cancelling either game, electing instead to split his team up.

That decision solved another problem. Under the conference's eligibility rules, Tech had three ineligible players. Cawthon sent the trio to play against New Mexico Normal.

The Arizona game was set for Friday night, Oct. 14. Seeking a large crowd for the conference opener, Cawthon declared "Ladies Night" with any escorted lady admitted free of charge. Fullback

RED RAIDERS

Harold Crites scored a pair of touchdowns to lead the Matadors to a 21-0 win.

As soon as the game ended, Cawthon boarded a train to lead his other squad in its road game against New Mexico Normal on Saturday. The strange weekend with its two games was a complete success as Tech won easily 43-7.

Some things in life are so strange their existence can't really be explained. How else can we account for the proliferation of tattoos, curling, tofu, the behavior of teenagers, and that some people go to bars hoping to meet the "right" person? Isn't it strange that someone can hear the life-altering message of salvation through Jesus Christ and just walk away from it?

And how strange is God's plan to save us? Think a minute about what God did. He could have come roaring down, destroying and blasting everyone whose sinfulness offended him, which, of course, is pretty much all of us. Then he could have brushed off his hands, nodded the divine head, and left a scorched planet in his wake. All in a day's work.

Instead, God came up with a totally novel plan: He would save the world by becoming a human being, letting himself be humiliated, tortured, and killed, thus establishing a kingdom of justice and righteousness that will last forever.

It's a strange way to save the world — but it's true.

It may sound strange, but many champions are made champions by setbacks.
— Olympic champion Bob Richards

**It's strange but true: God allowed himself
to be killed on a cross to save the world.**

PROVE IT!

Read Matthew 3:13-17.

"But John tried to deter him, saying, 'I need to be baptized by you, and do you come to me?'" (v. 14)

Big-time college recruiters weren't interested in Zach Thomas — and then he proved himself to Spike Dykes in one game.

Thomas is one of the greatest linebackers in Texas Tech history. From 1993-95, he was a three-year starter and was All-America his last two seasons. As a senior, he was the Southwest Conference Defensive Player of the Year.

Thomas is perhaps best remembered for one of the program's legendary plays. In the 14-7 upset of 8th-ranked Texas A&M in 1995, he returned an interception 23 yards for the game-winning touchdown with only 30 seconds left. Thomas played that day despite having a high fever all week. To prepare, he picked up every A&M tape he could find from the football offices and spent the week at home sick and watching game tapes. "There he sat, sick as a dog, watching game films all week," Dykes said. The star drew some serious ribbing from his teammates when his mother showed up to nurse him.

Thomas certainly proved himself in college. To even make it onto the Tech campus, though, he had to prove himself in high school. Big-time schools regarded him as a "slow-footed, undersized" player destined for some junior college. Tech's coaches were undecided as to whether they wanted him.

To settle the dispute, Dykes went to a playoff game to watch him. Thomas was limited by a badly sprained ankle, but he still managed to prove himself. The head coach returned convinced that Tech had to have him. "This guy, playing on a bad ankle, was the leading tackler and ball carrier," he said. "This is exactly the kind of kid we want."

Like Zach Thomas, we, too, have to prove ourselves over and over again in our lives. To our teachers, our bosses or supervisors, that person we'd like to date, to our parents. We shouldn't be surprised at this; Jesus was constantly besieged by those seeking a sign through which he would prove himself to them.

For us, it's always the same question: "Am I good enough?"

And yet, when it comes down to the most crucial situation in our lives, the answer is always a decisive and resounding "No!" Are we good enough to measure up to God? To deserve our salvation? John the Baptist knew he wasn't, and he was not only Jesus' relative but God's hand-chosen prophet. If he wasn't good enough, what chance do we have?

The notion that only "good" people can be church members is a perversion of Jesus' entire ministry. Nobody is good enough — without Jesus. Everybody is good enough — with Jesus. That's not because of anything we have done for God, but because of what he has done for us. We have nothing to prove to God.

Zach Thomas wasn't recruited a bunch. I'll tell you what: you can win games with a player like Zach Thomas.

— *Spike Dykes*

The bad news is we can't prove to God's satisfaction how good we are; the good news is that because of Jesus we don't have to.

DAY 67

STOP, THIEF!

Read Exodus 22:1-15.

"A thief must certainly make restitution" (v. 2b).

Tech and Washington still had some basketball to play, but they had a big problem: Some fan had stolen the game ball.

On Dec. 3, 2009, the 7-0 Red Raiders hosted the 5-0 and 10th-ranked Washington Huskies. The game was a thriller, tied at 80 with 4.8 seconds left. Junior forward Mike Singletary hit a running 3-pointer at the buzzer, and the students stormed the court in celebration. The ball bounced away under the Tech bench, and student manager Kevin Pierson fulfilled his basic mission of getting his hands on that ball.

Suddenly, though, an exuberant fan punched the ball from behind, snatched it up, and sprinted down the sideline with it, heading for an exit with his souvenir. Pierson dutifully gave chase but was hindered by the mob that milled about celebrating the big win. The fan and the ball escaped. Pierson's pursuit even made national television since *ESPN2* carried the game.

There was more confusion in store, however. The referees reviewed Singletary's shot and ruled he had not gotten it off before the buzzer sounded. The Raiders were in the locker room celebrating their win when they received a summons to return to the court. The game was still tied at 80 and was headed into overtime.

The fans and the debris they left behind had to be cleared before play could resume. A bigger problem loomed, though: the pilfered game ball. The student managers scrounged around and found a regulation game ball in a locker room, and the officials approved it for use in the game.

Tech then outscored the Huskies 19-12 in the extra period to win the game a second time, and the students dutifully repeated their rush onto the court. This time, Pierson latched onto the game ball and kept it safe from would-be thieves.

Buckle up your seat belt. Wear a bicycle or motorcycle helmet. Use your pooper scooper to clean up after your dog. Don't walk on the grass. Picky ordinances and picky laws in all their great abundance are an inescapable part of our modern lives.

When Moses came stumbling down Mt. Sinai after spending time as God's secretary, he brought with him a whole mess of laws and regulations, many of which undoubtedly seem picky to us today. What some of them provide, though, are practical examples of what for God is the basic principle underlying the theft of personal property: what is wrong must be made right.

While most of us today won't have to worry too much about the theft of livestock such as oxen, sheep, and donkeys, making what is wrong right remains a way of life for Christians. To get right with other people requires anything from restitution to apologies. To get right with God requires Jesus Christ.

I really thought my life was flashing before my eyes as I thought I'd lost the game ball from a huge game. I thought I was dead meat.
— *Tech student manager Kevin Pierson*

To make right the wrong of stealing requires restitution; to make right our relationship with God requires Jesus Christ.

DAY 68

WHAT A SURPRISE!

Read 1 Thessalonians 5:1-11.

"But you, brothers, are not in darkness so that this day should surprise you like a thief" (v. 4).

To no one's surprise, Texas Tech was an underdog against Texas Western. What happened surprised everyone.

The 1950 football season began for the Red Raiders just as about everyone expected. Coach Dell Morgan's team was young, so a rebuilding year was in order. It didn't help that four of the first five games were against teams from the Southwest Conference.

Sure enough, Tech lost all four of those games and also lost to West Texas State (today's West Texas A&M). So, not surprisingly, the 4-1 Texas Western Miners (today's Texas El-Paso) were favored to win when they rolled into Jones Stadium on Oct. 28.

Western promptly marched to a first down at the Raider 9 in the first quarter but fumbled on fourth and goal from the 1. Dick Jackson recovered for Tech to give the team what looked like a temporary reprieve. It was much more than that.

The game was scoreless into the second quarter, which became the most surprising period of the season. First, J.W. Thompson scored on a 3-yard run. Quarterback John Moughon then laid a 56-yard bomb into the hands of four-year letterman Elbert Johnson for another TD. Bobby Close gathered in the free kick following a safety and streaked 76 yards down the sideline for yet another score. The rout was on when quarterback Pete Edwards scored on a 1-yard plunge.

The third quarter was just as surprising. Dick Pirtle blocked a punt and Jackson took it 13 yards for a score. Sandy Welton scored twice on runs of 21 and 3 yards. Edwards scored again, this time from the 6, and then hit Welton with a 30-yard TD toss.

Surprisingly, Tech had scored 61 straight points before Western managed a late touchdown in the 61-7 rout.

Like an unexpected Tech win, surprise birthday parties are a delight. And what's the fun of opening Christmas presents when we already know what's in them? Some surprises in life provide us with experiences that are both joyful and delightful.

Generally, though, we expend energy and resources to avoid most surprises and the impact they may have upon our lives. We may be surprised by the exact timing of a baby's arrival, but we nevertheless have the bags packed beforehand and the nursery all set for its occupant. Paul used this very image (v. 3) to describe the Day of the Lord, when Jesus will return to claim his own and establish his kingdom. We may be caught by surprise, but we must still be ready.

The consequences of being caught unprepared by a baby's insistence on being born are serious indeed. They pale, however, beside the eternal effects of not being ready when Jesus returns. We prepare ourselves just as Paul told us to (v. 8): We live in faith, hope, and love, ever on the alert for that great, promised day.

Surprise me.
        — *Yogi Berra to his wife on where she should bury him*

**The timing of Jesus' return will be a surprise;
the consequences should not be.**

DAY 69

IN GOD'S OWN TIME

Read James 5:7-12.

"Be patient, then, brothers, until the Lord's coming" (v. 7).

Extraordinary patience kept B. J. Symons at Texas Tech. He was rewarded with one of the greatest single season any major college quarterback had ever had.

Symons was part of the last recruiting class signed in 1999 by head coach Spike Dykes. He was one of three quarterbacks in that bunch; the other two were Mickey Peters, who shifted to wide receiver successfully, and Nathan Chandler, who transferred and went on to start for Iowa. Symons stayed, and stayed, and stayed, languishing and learning and waiting for it all to pay off.

Symons waited fifty games before he ever started one at Tech. He was redshirted in 1999 and then found himself stuck behind Kliff Kingsbury for three seasons. He played in only seventeen games, completing 56 of 80 passes.

Not surprisingly, the thought of transferring often crossed his mind during the long wait. But just as quickly as he considered it, he discarded it. He simply enjoyed being at Tech. He also had no animosity toward Kingsbury, who was one of his best friends.

Symons did sometimes look longingly northward toward Norman. His head coach at Tech, Mike Leach, had recruited him for Oklahoma, which had been one of Symons' top choices. The team went through some uncertainty at quarterback after the 2000 national title season. "I feel like I probably would have had a good shot to be the starter after [2000]," Symons said.

So he stayed at Tech and patiently waited his turn. He finally got his shot as a senior in 2003. All he did was break the NCAA record for single-season passing yards with 5,833. He set Big 12 and school records with 48 touchdown passes in the 12-game regular season, breaking Kingsbury's record of 45.

B. J. Symons became "a poster boy for delayed gratification."

Have you ever left a restaurant because the server didn't take your order quickly enough? Complained at your doctor's office about waiting too long? Wondered how much longer a sermon was going to last?

It isn't just the machinations of the world with which we're impatient; we want God to move at our pace, not his. For instance, how often have you prayed and expected — indeed, demanded — an immediate answer from God? And aren't Christians the world over impatient for the glorious day when Jesus will return and set everything right? We're in a hurry but God obviously isn't.

As rare as it seems to be, patience is nevertheless included among the likes of gentleness, humility, kindness, and compassion as attributes of a Christian.

God expects us to be patient. He knows what he's doing; he is in control, and his will shall be done. On his schedule, not ours.

His patience and his dedication really paid off, and that's why he's doing as well as he is right now.
— Mike Leach on B. J. Symons in 2003

God moves in his own time, so often we must wait for him to act, remaining faithful and patient.

DAY 70

HAPPY DAYS

Read Nehemiah 8:1-3, 9-12.

"'Do not grieve, for the joy of the Lord is your strength'"
(v. 10b).

The Texas A&M Aggies were quite the happy lot when they trotted into the locker room at halftime at Jones Stadium. Their delight lasted until the second play from scrimmage of the last half.

The visiting boys from College Station felt pretty good at the break on Nov. 5, 2005. They trailed 16th-ranked Tech only 14-10 after falling behind early 14-0. Moreover, they were to receive the second-half kickoff. The plan was to score again and take the lead. More happiness.

Scratch that plan, along with any thoughts of leaving Lubbock all smiles after an upset. Free safety Dwayne Slay delivered one of his patented bone-crushing tackles on second down after the kickoff. The blow jarred the ball loose, and Antonio Huffman fell on it. Eight plays later, Tech scored. A rout was under way.

When the dust settled, the Red Raiders had scored touchdowns on six straight possessions. A&M managed a meaningless score in between all the carnage to put the final of 56-17 on the board.

Quarterback Cody Hodges lit up the A&M secondary for 408 passing yards and two touchdowns. Running back Taurean Henderson was quite happy too, after assembling 178 yards of total offense and scoring four times.

Hodges was at his happiest after a touchdown pass he didn't

throw. With 2:27 to play, senior inside receiver Slade Hodges, Cody's twin brother, caught the first touchdown pass of his career on a toss from backup Graham Harrell. "I'm more excited about that than anything of the night," Cody said. Overjoyed, he ran onto the field so quickly to high-five his brother that he thought for a moment he might draw a personal foul penalty. He didn't.

Overall, just about everybody was happy. Except the Aggies.

A widespread theology preaches that happiness and prosperity are signs of faithfulness. It's certainly seductive, this notion that with faith comes happiness.

But it reduces God to a servant or a vending machine existing only to meet our wishes, coughing up whatever it takes to make us happy. This theology also means that if I am not happy, then God has failed.

Yes, God wants us to be happy. God gave us our life to enjoy; God created this world for us to enjoy; he sure doesn't need it. In God's economy, though, we are to be happy but only with conditions. If it is sin that makes us happy, God doesn't want it for our lives. Moreover, if it is some thing in our lives, some circumstance in our lives, or even some person in our lives that makes us happy, then God is indifferent about it.

God is so good to us that he wants more for us than happiness, which is temporal and worldly. For us, he wants joy, which is eternal and divine. Joy is found only in God through Jesus Christ.

We were right where we wanted to be at halftime.
— A&M quarterback Reggie McNeal

Happiness simply isn't good enough for us
because it doesn't depend upon Jesus Christ.

DAY 71

RUN FOR IT

Read John 20:1-10.

"Peter and the other disciple started for the tomb. Both were running, but the other disciple outran Peter and reached the tomb first" (vv. 3-4).

The greatest cross-country runner in college history ran a race as a child to save a friend's life — and lost.

Texas Tech cross-country coach Jon Murray called what Sally Kipyego did for his program "revolutionary." From 2006-09, Kipyego ran for Tech with an excellence that may never be equaled. She won nine NCAA championships, running to more NCAA titles in two seasons than any other runner in history. She was the first woman to win three straight Division 1 cross-country titles and the first woman to win three straight Big 12 titles.

Kipyego wasn't born running, but she came pretty close. As a young girl, she ran more than 15 miles a day to attend school in her native Kenya. When she was 11, she made a run that determined the path of her life. Her older brother's best friend suffered a hard fall from his bicycle. Kipyego's job was to run get help at a clinic in the nearest village, which was more than seven miles away. When she arrived, the doctor refused to come treat her friend, ultimately locking the door to keep her out of the facility.

Close to hysterics, the youngster repeated her run, only to find her friend had worsened. All she could do was sit down and join her brother to watch the child die in their arms.

"I felt so helpless when I went through that," Kipyego said. "It's kind of haunted me to look back at that during the rest of my life." The tragedy inspired her to major in nursing at Tech with the goal of returning home to Kenya to help provide better health care there.

Keeping up with her schoolwork and her sport kept Kipyego running literally and figuratively during her years in Lubbock. Some days her rounds kept her on her feet for 12 hours, and then she still had her workout to take care of. She never slowed down.

Hit the ground running — every morning that's what you do as you leave the house and re-enter the rat race. You run errands; you run though a presentation; you give someone a run for his money; you always want to be in the running and never run-of-the-mill.

You're always running toward something, such as your goals, or away from something, such as your past. Many of us spend much of our lives foolishly attempting to run away from God, the purposes he has for us, and the blessings he is waiting to give us.

No matter how hard or how far you run, though, you can never outrun yourself or God. God keeps pace with you, calling you in the short run to take care of the long run by falling to your knees and running for your life — to Jesus — just as Peter and the other disciple ran that first Easter morning.

On your knees, you run all the way to glory.

She [took] both the cross country and track teams to heights we've never been.

— Coach Jon Murray on Sally Kipyego

You can run to eternity by going to your knees.

FAITHFUL LIVES

Read Hebrews 11:1-12.

"Faith is the substance of things hoped for, the evidence of things not seen" (v. 1 NKJV).

In a different day and age, Tech head coach Jim Carlen openly hired coaches who were Christians and requested that his players practice their faith.

JT King stepped down as Tech's head football coach after the 1969 season. As athletic director, he then led the search for his successor. He was thorough, personally interviewing 49 candidates and talking on the phone to about 150 coaches. Carlen, the head coach at West Virginia, was the man he wanted.

The new boss Raider hit town in 1970 and headed up the Tech program for five seasons. He guided his squads to bowl games in four of those years, wining two of them. His best season was 1973 when the Raiders went 11-1 (tying the school record for wins in a season) and beat Tennessee 28-19 in the Gator Bowl.

Carlen was open and public about his faith. In April 2011, he said he was one of the original six members of the Fellowship of Christian Athletes; he was active in the organization throughout his coaching career. He once said, "When I hired a coach, I always took a close look at his spiritual life."

A lay preacher, Carlen had three inviolate rules for his players. "My coaches and I discuss them thoroughly with the boys and their parents before we ever sign them," he said. Rule No. 1: Get to church every Sunday, the church of your choice. Rule No. 2: No smoking and drinking. Rule No. 3: No class cuts. None at all.

Carlen said that if parents told him they wanted their son to attend church, he saw that the player did. "I don't demand that every boy attend, but I do request it," he said.

The student underground newspaper tagged Carlen with the somewhat less-than-flattering nickname "Morality Fats." As a result, he lost some weight, not his faith.

Like Jim Carlen, your faith forms the heart and soul of what you are. Faith in people, things, ideologies, and concepts to a large extent determines how you spend your life. You believe in the Red Raiders, in your family, in the basic goodness of Americans, in freedom and liberty, and in abiding by the law. These beliefs mold you and make you the person you are.

This is all great stuff, of course, that makes for decent human beings and productive lives. None of it, however, is as important as what you believe about Jesus. To have faith in Jesus is to believe his message of hope and salvation as recorded in the Bible. True faith in Jesus, however, has an additional component; it must also include a personal commitment to him. In other words, you don't just believe in Jesus; you live for him.

Faith in Jesus does more than shape your life; it determines your eternity.

When you have God on your side, you don't have to worry.
— Jim Carlen

Your belief system is the foundation
upon which you build a life; faith in Jesus
is the foundation for your eternal life.

DAY 73

SMART MOVE

Read 1 Kings 4:29-34; 11:1-6 .

"[Solomon] was wiser than any other man. . . . As Solomon grew old, his wives turned his heart after other gods, and his heart was not fully devoted to the Lord his God" (vv. 4:31, 11:4).

Mike Leach's call seemed like such a bad move that his quarterback questioned it. It was such a smart move, however, that it completed the greatest comeback in Tech history to that point.

Kansas simply blew the Red Raiders out of the stadium in the first half on Sept. 25, 2004. Only a week after Tech came from 21 points down to beat TCU — tying the record for biggest comeback — the Raiders trailed KU 30-5 with 48 seconds left in the second quarter. Not many Raider fans were thinking comeback this time.

Still, a little hope stirred when the Raiders ended the half by driving 80 yards in 33 seconds. Trey Haverty caught a 32-yard TD toss from Sonny Cumbie. The 2-point conversion failed.

Then on the Jayhawks' first possession of the last half, Chad Johnson nabbed an interception that set up Taurean Henderson's 1-yard touchdown run. At 30-18, the game had gotten very interesting. It got downright exciting when Cumbie connected with Jarrett Hicks on a 27-yard touchdown late in the third quarter.

The comeback stalled after that, though, with the score staying at 30-24 deep into the fourth quarter. Tech faced third-and-6 from its own 30 with only 2:37 left when Leach made his smart move that didn't seem so smart at first. He called a simple handoff up the middle to Henderson. "He kind of took us all by surprise, making that call," Cumbie said.

With Kansas expecting a pass and dropping eight players into coverage, Henderson ran straight up the gut virtually untouched for 70 yards. "I saw daylight, and I hit it," he said.

The smart move and the extra point gave Tech a 31-30 lead that held up when Jabari Smith got an interception two plays later.

Remember that time you wrecked the car when you spilled hot coffee on your lap? That cold morning you fell out of the boat? The time you gave your honey a tool box for her birthday?

Formal education notwithstanding, we all make some dumb moves sometimes because time spent in a classroom is not an accurate gauge of common sense. Folks impressed with their own smarts often grace us with erudite pronouncements that we intuitively recognize as flawed, unworkable, or simply wrong.

A good example is the observation that great intelligence and scholarship are inherently incompatible with a deep and abiding faith in God. That is, the more we know, the less we believe. Any incompatibility occurs, however, only because we begin to trust in our own wisdom rather than the wisdom of God. We forget, as Solomon did, that God is the ultimate source of all our knowledge and wisdom and that even our ability to learn is a gift from God.

Not smart at all.

I had to check with [Mike Leach] to make sure that's what he wanted.
— Sonny Cumbie on his coach's smart call

**Being truly smart means trusting in God's
wisdom rather than only in our own knowledge.**

YOU DECIDE

Read Luke 4:16-30.

"They got up, drove him out of the town, and took him to the brow of the hill . . . to throw him down the cliff" (v. 29).

Ivory McCann made a simply awful decision — and it was just what Texas Tech needed.

McCann's decision was so bad that when he made it, the groan of the Jones Stadium crowd was audible. Tech special teams coach Manny Matsakis screamed on the sideline, "No, no, no."

So what did the true freshman do in his first-ever college game that was so horrible? He fielded a kickoff 8 yards deep in the left corner of the end zone — and he decided to bring it out.

In the 2001 season opener, the Red Raiders found themselves getting a tougher battle than they expected from New Mexico. The home team led only 21-14 at halftime, and a third-quarter field goal cut the lead to four. On the subsequent kickoff, McCann made his bad decision.

As sportswriter Jeremy Cowen put it, "Against the wishes of his coaches, his teammates — heck, the whole darned stadium — McCann wheeled out of the end zone." As he did so, "it didn't take long for the 'uh-ohs' visibly heard around the stadium to turn into 'oohs' and 'ahs.'" Or for Matsakis to change his screams to "Go, go, go!"

One of the team's fastest players, McCann sprinted out of the end zone and eluded a gang of Lobos around the 20. When he hit the 30, McCann was running alone. He juked his way past the New Mexico kicker at the Lobo 45 and coasted the rest of the way for a school-record 108-yard kickoff return.

"That play turned the entire game around," said senior strong safety Paul McClendon, who returned a fumble 54 yards for a fourth-quarter score that put the game away. That came after a screen pass Ricky Williams turned into a 33-yard touchdown.

Tech won 42-30, a win propelled by McCann's bad decision.

As with Ivory McCann, the decisions you have made along the way have shaped your life at every pivotal moment. Some decisions you made suddenly and carelessly; some you made carefully and deliberately; some were forced upon you. You may have discovered that some of those spur-of-the-moment decisions have turned out better than your carefully considered ones.

Of all your life's decisions, however, none is more important than one you cannot ignore: What have you done with Jesus? Even in Jesus' time and in his hometown, people chose to follow him or to reject him, and nothing has changed. The decision must still be made and nobody can make it for you. Ignoring Jesus won't work either; that is, in fact, a decision, and neither he nor the consequences of your decision will go away.

Carefully considered or spontaneous — how you arrive at a decision for Jesus doesn't matter. All that matters is that you get there.

I don't know if I was as much a fan of the decision as I was the return.
— Mike Leach

A decision for Jesus may be spontaneous or
considered; what counts is that you make it.

BIG DEAL

Read Ephesians 3:1-13.

"His intent was that now, through the church, the manifold wisdom of God should be made known" (v. 10).

You would think a Red Raider's dropping the ball a half-yard shy of the game-winning touchdown would be a big deal for the other team. As it turned out, it was a big deal for Tech.

With 1,103 yards in 2014, junior DeAndre Washington became Tech's first 1,000-yard rusher since Ricky Williams in 1998. As a senior, he led the Big 12 with 1,492 yards. He finished his Tech career fifth on the Red Raiders' all-time rushing list.

Thus, much of Washington's time in Lubbock was a big deal for Tech's football fortunes. He once, though, was the catalyst for a big play that appeared to be a disaster for Tech.

The 2-0 Red Raiders hosted 24th-ranked TCU on Sept. 12, 2013, in a rare Thursday night game. With less than four minutes to play, the game was tied at 10. Backup quarterback Davis Webb, in the game because of an injury to freshman starter Baker Mayfield, completed a pass to Washington, who broke open down the sideline. It was a sure-fire 49-yard touchdown that looked like a game winner. Celebrating too early, though, Washington tossed the ball away at the half-yard line.

"I just want to say it was a dumb mistake on my part," Washington said. Head coach Kliff Kingsbury's reaction to what was truly a big deal was as interesting as the play itself: He treated it like no big deal at all. He told Washington, "Hey, man, it happens" and simply said to his offense, "We've got to go score again."

Strangely, the play didn't turn out to be a game-saving big deal for TCU. Because the ball didn't roll out of the end zone, the refs awarded Tech a touchdown rather than giving TCU a touchback. They did, however, flag the team for excessive celebration. Thus, Tech got the ball at the 15. Three plays later with 3:48 on the clock, Webb found junior wide receiver Bradley Marquez for a 19-yard touchdown pass. A late field goal made the final score 20-10.

Like Tech wins over ranked teams such as TCU, "big deals" are important components of our lives. A wedding, childbirth, a new job, a new house, even a new car. In many ways, what we regard as a big deal is what shapes not only our lives but our character.

One of the most unfathomable anomalies of faith in America today is that while many people profess to be die-hard Christians, they disdain involvement with a local church. As Paul tells us, however, the Church is a very big deal to God; it is at the heart of his redemptive work; it is a vital part of his eternal purposes.

The Church is no accident of history. It isn't true that Jesus died on the cross and all he wound up with for his troubles was the stinking Church. It is no consolation prize.

Rather, the Church is the primary instrument through which God's plan of cosmic and eternal salvation is worked out. And it doesn't get any bigger than that.

Not a big deal. Go make a play.
    — Kliff Kingsbury after DeAndre Washington's gaffe vs. TCU

**To disdain church involvement is to assert
that God doesn't know what he's doing.**

DAY 76

ON CALL

Read 1 Samuel 3:1-18.

"The Lord came and stood there, calling as at the other times, 'Samuel! Samuel!' Then Samuel said, 'Speak, for your servant is listening'" (v. 10).

James Hadnot reluctantly answered his coach's call to switch positions. As a result, he became a record-setting star.

Hadnot spent his first two seasons in Lubbock as a rather unproductive tight end. Still, he had no intentions of giving up the position. "I thought I was always going to finish as a tight end," he said. His goal was to break Andre Tillman's receiving records for a tight end at Tech.

As the 1978 season neared, though, head coach Rex Dockery had other ideas, born largely of desperation. His offense needed a running back badly, and when he looked at Hadnot, he saw a 6-foot-3, 245-lb. player who was pretty much being wasted. So, only two weeks before the opener against Southern Cal, Hadnot answered his coach's call and made the move.

"It was a lot of stuff I had to grasp," Hadnot said, and it took him a while to get comfortable at his new position. He exploded out of nowhere the fifth game of the season against New Mexico when he set a school record with 268 yards rushing on 26 carries in the 36-23 win.

Hadnot's most memorable moment came in the tenth game of the '78 season against 6th-ranked Houston. Quarterback Ron

Reeves capped a 72-yard drive with a 1-yard run with 3:40 to play to pull Tech to within 21-20. Dockery went for two and called for a screen pass to Hadnot. "He broke three, four, five tackles," Reeves recalled. "I'd like to see the play again to count 'em up." The pass and the 22-21 win became part of Texas Tech lore.

In his two seasons in the backfield, Hadnot set a school rushing record with 2,794 yards and led the Southwest Conference in rushing both years. He was the league's Offensive Player of the Year twice. He was taken in the third round of the NFL draft and was admitted to Tech's Hall of Honor in 2005.

A team player is someone who does whatever the coach calls upon him to do for the good of the team. Something quite similar occurs when God places a specific call upon a Christian's life.

This is much scarier, though, than shifting positions on a football team as James Hadnot did. All too many folks believe that answering God's call means going into the ministry, packing the family up, and moving to the other side of the world to some place where folks have never heard of air conditioning, sirloin steaks, paved roads, or the Red Raiders. Zambia. Chile. Somewhere in the Far East like Laos.

Not for you, no thank you. And who can blame you?

But God usually calls folks to serve him where they are. In fact, God put you where you are right now, and he has a purpose in placing you there. Wherever you are, you are called to serve him.

You don't see a lot of people move from tight end to running back.
  — Tech quarterback Ron Reeves on James Hadnot's position switch

God calls you to serve him right now
right where he has put you, wherever that is.

DAY 77

TEN TO REMEMBER

Read Exodus 20:1-17.

"God spoke all these words: 'I am the Lord your God . . . .
You shall have no other gods before me'" (vv. 1, 3).

Texas Tech head coach Pete Cawthon had his own version of
The Ten Commandments.

Cawthon coached the Red Raiders from 1930-40 and won 76
games, a school record that held up until Spike Dykes won 82
games from 1986-99. (Mike Leach won 84 games during his
tenure.) Cawthon's 10-2 team of 1932 was the country's highest
scoring squad. His 1937 team went to the Sun Bowl, the program's
first-ever bowl game, and his 1938 team went 10-0 and wound up
in the Cotton Bowl. That '37 squad became one of the first major
college football teams to fly to a game when it took a plane to play
the University of Detroit.

Cawthon was a severe disciplinarian. He once removed all the
soap from the shower room "so the players would smell as bad
as they looked." He told his players "you either loves the game or
the goils [girls]. Take a choice."

He posted a set of rules and regulations in the dressing room
and the dormitory and expected them to be followed to the letter.
Since there were ten of them, the players jokingly referred to the
regulations as the Ten Commandments.

Cawthon's Ten Commandments read as follows: 1) Eat regular
and that which will agree with you. 2) Use no tobacco in any form.

3) Eat sugar as prescribed by the coaches individually. 4) Go to bed by eleven o'clock each and every night except the night before the game and then be in bed by ten o'clock. 5) Watch your digestion very closely. 6) Get out early when possible. 7) Do not eat between meals. 8) Pass all your courses. 9) No liquor or dances. 10) Drink water freely between meals — very little at meals — and don't drink water for twenty minutes after your workout and little at that.

Just like Peter Cawthon's ten rules for his players to remember, you have your list and you're ready to go. You may have to fetch a gallon of paint and a water hose from the hardware store; chips, peanuts, and sodas from the grocery store for watching tonight's football game with your buddies; the tickets for the band concert. Your list helps you remember.

God also made a list once of things he wanted you to remember; it's called the Ten Commandments. Just as your list reminds you to do something, so does God's list remind you of how you are to act in your dealings with other people and with him. A life dedicated to Jesus is a life devoted to relationships, and God's list emphasizes that the social life and the spiritual life of the faithful cannot be sundered. God's relationship to you is one of unceasing, unqualified love, and you are to mirror that divine love in your relationships with others. In case you forget, you have a list.

These rules and regulations are for you. . . . Live by them and be a real man and football player — disobey them and be a big jelly and a wisher.
— The postscript to Pete Cawthon's Ten Commandments

God's list is a set of instructions on how you are to conduct yourself with other people and with him.

JUST PERFECT

Read Matthew 5:43-48.

"Be perfect, therefore, as your heavenly Father is perfect"
(v. 48).

For fifteen passes, Seth Doege was perfect. Not even lightning could stop him. After that — well, he was pretty close to perfect.

Against New Mexico on Sept. 17, 2011, Doege, a junior on his way to a record-setting career, completed his first pass of the game, a 14-yarder to receiver Eric Ward. Three plays later, he completed his fourth pass, and Darrin Moore took it to the end zone for a 56-yard touchdown. With less than 90 seconds gone in the game, Doege was a perfect 4-for-4. He was just getting warmed up.

On Tech's second possession, Doege hit five straight passes, the last one a 7-yard TD to Moore. He ran his streak to 11 straight before the New Mexico weather temporarily stalled him. With 3:50 left in the first quarter, a lightning delay sent the teams scurrying for cover for 51 minutes. Doege passed the time "having conversations with my teammates" and "staying focused and understanding what we're here to do."

Back on the field, he hit four more to run his completion streak to 15 before a receiver dropped a would-be touchdown on a perfectly thrown ball on a fade route. The string of completions tied the school record set by Taylor Potts in 2010.

Doege kept on throwing. Shortly before the end of the third quarter, he completed a screen pass to Tramain Swindall. Head coach Tommy Tuberville then took him out of the game, having left him in for that last pass. The completion left Doege 40-of-44 for the game, a percentage of 90.9, which set a new NCAA completion percentage mark for at least 40 pass attempts. The previous record holder was none other than Kliff Kingsbury.

Doege threw for 401 yards and five touchdowns in the 59-13 Tech win. He wasn't perfect, but he was awfully close.

Nobody's perfect; we all make mistakes every day. We botch our personal relationships; at work we seek competence, not perfection. To insist upon personal or professional perfection in our lives is to establish an impossibly high standard that will eventually destroy us physically, emotionally, and mentally.

Yet that is exactly the standard God sets for us. Our love is to be perfect, never ceasing, never failing, never qualified — just the way God loves us. And Jesus didn't limit his command to preachers and goody-two-shoes types. All of his disciples are to be perfect as they navigate their way through the world's ambiguous definition and understanding of love.

But that's impossible! Well, not necessarily, if to love perfectly is to serve God wholeheartedly and to follow Jesus with single-minded devotion. Anyhow, in his perfect love for us, God makes allowance for our imperfect love and the consequences of it in the perfection of Jesus.

If we chase perfection, we can catch excellence.

— *Vince Lombardi*

**In his perfect love for us, God provides a way
for us to escape the consequences
of our imperfect love for him: Jesus.**

BLESS YOU

Read Romans 5:1-11.

"We also rejoice in our sufferings because we know that suffering produces perseverance; perseverance, character; and character, hope. And hope does not disappoint us" (vv. 3-5a).

Matt Mooney survived injuries, transfers and a total transformation with his defense to become a key component of the most successful basketball team in Tech history. Asked by his mom how he felt about all that, Mooney had one word to say: "Blessed."

The Red Raiders of 2018-19 went 31-7, the most wins in school history, and advanced to the championship game in the NCAA Tournament for the first time ever. A shooting guard, Mooney was "a main factor in Tech's unprecedented season."

Mooney's one-word description of being blessed came after a win over top-seeded Gonzaga in the Elite Eight as he looked back over the twisting road he traveled down to get to that moment.

The Air Force Academy was the only school to offer him a D-1 scholarship. He accepted it, but the summer before he arrived in Colorado, he broke a leg and tore a ligament in a bicycle accident. Even after he rehabbed his injuries, Mooney realized the academy wasn't a good fit. He struggled with the hazing from upperclassmen and how little time he had to concentrate on basketball. He told one of his former high school coaches, "I jumped out of a helicopter, but I wanted to be in the gym."

So he transferred to South Dakota, his decision sealed by head coach Craig Smith's 10-page handwritten note. He became the team's featured star after scoring 31 points in his first-ever game.

After two seasons, though, Mooney told Smith, "Coach, I won't be able to live with myself if I don't get to the NCAA Tournament." This time, Mooney was in high demand, but Tech's Chris Beard sold him on the Red Raider program.

So after all that, there he was, on a ride that ended in the national title game. Matt Mooney was blessed and he knew it.

We just never know what God is up to. We can know, though, that he's always busy preparing blessings for us and that if we trust and obey him, he will pour out those blessings upon us.

Like Matt Mooney's injuries and struggles, it's hard sometime to find the blessing at the moment. That's often true in our own lives, too, and it is only after we can look back upon what we have endured that we understand it as a blessing as Matt Mooney did.

The key lies in trusting God, in realizing that God isn't out to destroy us but instead is interested only in doing good for us. That may even include allowing us to endure the consequences of a difficult lesson. God doesn't manage a candy store; more often, he relates to us as a stern but always loving parent.

If we truly love and trust God, no matter what our situation is now, he has blessings in store for us. This, above all, is our greatest hope.

Classic Matthew.
  — Matt Mooney's mom, Angela, on his answer about being blessed

Life's hardships are often transformed into blessings when we endure them trusting in God.

DAY 80

COMEBACK KIDS

Read Luke 23:26-43.

"Jesus answered him, 'I tell you the truth, today you will be with me in paradise'" (v. 43).

A team with less character might have decided it was time to wait for next season. Not the Red Raiders. Instead, they pulled off the greatest comeback in school and college bowl history.

Tech head coach Mike Leach told his team at halftime of the 2006 Insight Bowl that they had a chance to make history. That's because his team trailed by four touchdowns. It got worse.

When Minnesota kicked a field goal with 7:47 left in the third quarter, the Golden Gophers led 38-7. Any thoughts of a comeback seemed ludicrous at the time — except to the Tech players and the coaches. The Red Raiders proceeded to score 31 unanswered points in less than 20 minutes to send the game into overtime.

The record-setting comeback began with 4:58 left in the third period when sophomore quarterback Graham Harrell hit All-Big 12 wide receiver Joel Filani with a 43-yard TD pass. Harrell, the game's MVP, would throw for 445 yards and two touchdowns.

Then, in rapid succession, came an 8-yard scoring toss to wide receiver Robert Johnson and 1-yard touchdown runs from Harrell and sophomore running back Shannon Woods. With 2:39 to play, the Raiders trailed only 38-35 — but they still trailed.

They used their time outs and the defense forced a punt. With 1:06 left, Harrell and his gang got one last shot at completing the comeback when they took over at the own 11. Eight plays later, Alex Trlica, who set an NCAA record by converting 233 straight PATs, tied the game with a booming 52-yard field goal as the clock ticked down to all zeros.

In overtime, Minnesota got a field goal on its opening possession before Woods scored from the 3 for a 44-41 Tech win. The 31-point comeback made history, breaking the previous college bowl record of 30 points set by Marshall in the GMAC Bowl in 2001.

Life will have its setbacks whether they result from personal failures or from forces and people beyond your control. Being a Christian and a faithful follower of Jesus Christ doesn't insulate you from getting into deep trouble. Maybe financial problems suffocated you. A serious illness sidelined you. Or your family was hit with a great tragedy.

Life is a series of victories and defeats. Winning isn't about avoiding defeat; it's about getting back up to compete again. It's about making a comeback of your own.

When you avail yourself of God's grace and God's power, your comeback is always greater than your setback. You are never too far behind, and it's never too late in life's game for Jesus to lead you to victory, to turn trouble into triumph. As it was with the Red Raiders of 2006 and the thief on the cross who repented, it's not how you start that counts; it's how you finish.

I knew it was kind of a big one. I would have liked to have spotted them [fewer] points in order to come back from behind to win this thing.
— Mike Leach on the record-setting comeback vs. Minnesota

In life, victory is truly a matter of how you finish and whether you finish with Jesus at your side.

DAY 81

THE GOOD OLD DAYS

Read Psalm 102.

"My days vanish like smoke; . . . but you remain the same, and your years will never end" (vv. 3, 27).

The earliest times of the Texas Tech football program hardly constituted "the good old days."

From the outset, E. Y. Freeland, Tech's first head football coach, had trouble finding a suitable place to practice. His basic problem was the campus terrain, which was "a sea of goat grass, thistles, cat's claws and other weeds sharp enough to puncture the hide of the toughest football player." A vacant lot just off the campus served as the first practice field in 1925 before the head coach was able to find a more permanent site. Even this location, however, didn't leave the players reminiscing about the good old days.

A garage apartment at the end of Broadway and the campus was the team's dressing room. The garage had been left behind when a house on the lot had been cleared to make way for the first campus construction. P. C. "Preacher" Callaway, an end on the first Tech team, recalled that each day after the team dressed for practice, the players "would jog the four or five blocks to the other side of 19th to a brier patch" for workouts. Every day, Callaway recalled, "Coach Freeland and [assistant] coach [Grady] Higginbotham would climb in Freeland's car and drive out to the practice field. The team would trot along behind."

Those pioneer football players didn't have the luxury of a

beautiful home stadium either. They played their first games at the South Plains Fair Ground in part because, as Callaway put it, "there were fewer grass burrs and goat heads" than on the Tech campus. At halftime, the teams gathered in tents that had been pitched at either end of the playing field.

Conditions improved in 1926 with a dedicated field on the north side of the campus. Not until 1927, though, was Tech Field with its real bleachers ready for play and what might be considered some honest-to-goodness "good old days" could begin.

It's a brutal truth that time just never stands still. The current of your life sweeps you along until you realize one day you've lived long enough to have a past. Part of it you cling to fondly. The stunts you pulled with your high-school buddies. Your first apartment. That dance with your first love. That special vacation. Those "good old days."

You hold on relentlessly to the memory of those old, familiar ways because of the stability they provide in our uncertain world. They will always be there even as times change and you age.

Another constant exists in your life too. God has been a part of every event in your life that created a memory because he was there. He's always there with you; the question is whether you ignore him or make him a part of your day.

A "good old day" is any day shared with God.

The conditions under which those first [Texas Tech] football players practiced and played would seem almost barbaric [today].
— *Ralph Sellmeyer and James Davidson in* The Red Raiders

**Today is one of the "good old days"
if you share it with God.**

DAY 82

HEART AND SOUL

Read Romans 12:1-2.

"Therefore, I urge you, brothers, in view of God's mercy, to offer your bodies as living sacrifices, holy and pleasing to God — this is your spiritual act of worship" (v. 1).

Even major heart surgery couldn't keep Spike Dykes from honoring a commitment he had made.

The Texas Tech legend once declared that he existed "on the four basic food groups: fried chicken, pizza, chicken-fried steak with cream gravy, and ice cream." He noted that "if you grow up in West Texas, you get chicken-fried steak before you get pablum."

In other words, Dykes did not exactly live a healthful lifestyle, especially at the dinner table. Not surprisingly, therefore, the results of his annual physical in the summer of 1997 were not too good. The coach's heart surgeon told him that he needed surgery — immediately. He had six bypasses "just to get around all the chicken fried steak and cream gravy they found in there."

That was not Dykes' first brush with heart problems. In the fall of 1996, he had surgery to take care of some blockage. He had the procedure done on Sunday morning after a 31-3 win over Oklahoma State on Saturday. "Nobody ever knew about it, and I was back that afternoon for our workout and films," Dykes said.

Perhaps the most dramatic example of the coach's commitment to the promises he made came after he retired. He had major heart surgery again and had promised to give a speech to, as his son,

Rick, put it, "a group of electrical co-op workers in a little-bitty town called Muleshoe, Texas, on Thursday night." Dad coerced his son into getting him out of the hospital — against his doctor's orders — and driving him to the meeting.

"Anybody else in the world would have cancelled that engagement," Rick said. "Dad not only felt he had to go; he wanted to spend the entire meeting with those people, too."

When you stood in a church and recited your wedding vows, did you make a decision that you could walk away from when things got tough, or did you make a lifelong commitment? Is your job just a way to get a paycheck, or are you committed to it?

Commitment seems almost a dirty word in our society these days, a synonym for chains, an antonym for freedom. Perhaps this is why so many people are afraid of Jesus: Jesus demands commitment. To speak of offering yourself as "a living sacrifice" is not to speak blithely of making a decision but of heart-body-mind-and-soul commitment.

But commitment actually means "purpose and meaning," especially when you're talking about your life. Commitment makes life worthwhile. Anyway, in insisting upon commitment, Jesus isn't asking anything from you that he hasn't already given to you himself. His commitment to you was so deep that he died for you.

If you say you're going to do something, you need to do it.

— *Spike Dykes*

**Rather than constraining you, commitment
to Jesus lends meaning to your life,
releasing you to move forward with purpose.**

DREAM WORLD

Read Joshua 3.

"All Israel passed by until the whole nation had completed the crossing on dry ground" (v. 17b).

All Jackson Richards ever dreamed of growing up was playing football for Texas Tech.

In this age of cutthroat recruiting with commitments that often have the life span of smoke, Richards' experience was a rarity. He was a four-star defensive end rated number-three at his position in Texas and 25th nationally. Schools from LSU to Texas A&M all wanted him. Yet, his recruitment didn't amount to much.

That's because Richards declared his commitment to Texas Tech when he was a 16-year-old sophomore. That was nearly two years before his graduating class could officially sign and more than two years before he could enroll in college.

"He didn't grow up in West Texas, but he's about as West Texas as he can be," his father said. In other words, Richards has been "as scarlet and black as they come for as long as he can remember."

When Mike Leach was fired as the Texas Tech head coach during Richards' senior year of high school, A&M's coaches saw an opening and swooped in. They persuaded Richards to make an official visit to Aggieland, and he was impressed by what he saw. "Everything about that school was just great," he said. "The facilities were amazing. I loved all the coaches."

But he "couldn't get past one thought: the idea of putting on that A&M helmet and playing against Texas Tech." "I remember growing up," Richards said, "and being at the grandparents' house who lived in Lubbock with my family who either went to Tech or were big Tech fans."

Jackson Richards' dream came true in 2010 when he arrived in Lubbock as a Red Raider. After a redshirt season, that dream played out from 2011-14 when he saw action in 48 of Tech's 60 games, 28 of them as a starter.

No matter how tightly or doggedly we cling to our dreams, devotion to them won't make them a reality. Moreover, the cold truth is that all too often dreams don't come true even when we put forth a mighty effort. The realization of dreams generally results from a head-on collision of persistence and timing.

But what if our dreams don't come true because they're not the same dreams God has for us? That is, they're not good enough and, in many cases, they're not big enough.

God calls us to great achievements because God's dreams for us are greater than our dreams for ourselves. Could the Israelites, wallowing in the misery of slavery, even dream of a land of their own? Could they imagine actually going to such a place?

The fulfillment of such great dreams occurs only when our dreams and God's will for our lives are the same. Our dreams should be worthy of our best — and worthy of God's involvement in making them come true.

It's just the culture I grew up in.
— Jackson Richards on why he dreamed of being a Red Raider

If our dreams are to come true, they must be worthy of God's involvement in them.

DAY 84

SIZE MATTERS

Read Luke 19:1-10.

"[Zacchaeus] wanted to see who Jesus was, but being a short man he could not, because of the crowd. So he ran ahead and climbed a sycamore-fig tree to see him" (vv. 3-4).

On the football field, size matters; it's always the bigger the better. Except, that is, in the case of Tyrone Thurman.

In 2002, Thurman was inducted into the Texas Tech Hall of Honor. He was a four-year letterman (1985-88) whose specialty was returning punts. He led the Southwest Conference in punt returns three times, and his senior season the Associated Press named him to its All-America first team as a kick returner.

His 96-yard return in the 23-21 defeat of Texas in 1986 still stands as the school record. In the 27-21 upset of 15th-ranked Texas A&M in 1987, Thurman followed blocks by Monty Melcher and James Mosley down the sideline for a 74-yard touchdown only 85 seconds into the game.

Thurman even played some for coach Gerald Myers' basketball team. Myers offered Thurman a chance to play against Texas and Arkansas to help the Raiders break their press. He played and had ten assists in an upset of the nationally ranked Razorbacks.

Despite his obvious abilities, Thurman wasn't highly recruited out of high school. Why? Because he was only 5-foot-3 and 130 pounds, the smallest player in college football at the time. His

Tech teammates nicknamed him "Smurf" for obvious reasons.

Thurman always declared that his favorite play came in the 33-32 win over Texas in 1988. With time running out and Texas ahead, the Raiders faced fourth-and-one. Thurman went in as a pass receiver and ran the short route. He caught the pass but was hit short of the first down. All 5-foot-3 and 130 lbs. of him broke the tackle and battled for the first down. Tech scored the game winner on the next play.

Bigger is better! Such is one of the most powerful mantras of our time. We expand our football stadiums. We augment our body parts. Hey, make that a triple cheeseburger and a large order of fries! My company is bigger than your company. Even our church buildings must be bigger to be better. About the only exception to our all-consuming drive for bigness is our waistlines.

But size obviously didn't matter to Jesus. After all, salvation came to the house of an evil tax collector who was so short he had to climb a tree to catch a glimpse of our Lord. Zacchaeus indeed had a big bank account; he was a big man in town even if his own people scorned him. But none of that — including Zacchaeus' height — mattered; Zacchaeus received salvation because of his repentance, which revealed itself in a changed life.

The same is true for us today. What matters is the size of the heart devoted to our Lord.

When people question my ability because of my height, I take that as a challenge. It pushes me harder.
— *Tyrone Thurman*

**Size matters to Jesus, but only the size
of the heart of the one who would follow Him.**

DAY 85

AD MAN

Read Mark 1:21-28.

"News about him spread quickly over the whole region"
(v. 28).

Jack Dale learned early on that it pays to advertise.

"We didn't always have the best team, but we always had the best announcer." So declared legendary Texas Tech men's basketball coach and athletic director Gerald Myers on Dale, a fixture on Lubbock radio for more than fifty years. Dale began his broadcasting career in Lubbock in 1952 and was the voice for more than 1,300 Red Raider basketball games until his retirement in 2003. He also broadcast 47 seasons of Tech football through 1999.

John Harris, color analyst for Tech football broadcasts starting in 1982, said that Dale always had his Bible with him. He recalled that often they'd be sitting and waiting for their flight to take off, "and I always joked that I was reading *Sports Illustrated* and Jack was reading the Bible. He might have known something that I didn't know."

What Dale also knew early on in his life was that he wanted to be a sportscaster. He called imaginary games to himself as a farm boy driving a tractor in Kansas. After high school, he spent six months at a Kansas City radio trade school.

Then he faced a dilemma: What to do now since he was stuck on a farm far, far away from any sports markets? His answer was to advertise. He sent letters to 113 stations in the fall of 1952 and landed the job in Lubbock that December.

Dale insisted God — and not his talent — got him the position. "Listen, I'm telling you, all this was ordained," he said in 2002. "I sent them a tape of a game that I did in Topeka, Kansas, that had to be the worst portrayal of a football game that anybody had ever done or anybody had ever listened to."

Dale's typical modesty may have been at work, but so was his advertising campaign.

Commercials and advertisements for products, goods, and services inundate us. Watch NASCAR: Decals cover the cars and the drivers' uniforms. Turn on your computer: Ads pop up. TV, radio, newspapers, billboards, every square inch of every wall — everyone's one trying to get the word out the best way possible.

Jesus was no different in that he used the most effective and efficient means of advertising he had at his disposal to spread his message of salvation and hope among the masses. That was word of mouth.

In his ministry, Jesus didn't isolate himself; instead, he moved from town to town among the common folks, preaching, teaching, and healing. Those who encountered Jesus then told others about their experience, thus spreading the news about the good news. Almost two millennia later, nothing's really changed. Speaking to someone else about Jesus remains the best way to get the word out, and the best advertisement of all is a changed life.

It was ordained for me to come to KFYO in Lubbock.
— Jack Dale on how he landed his broadcasting job

The best advertising for Jesus is word of mouth, telling others what he has done for you.

DAY 86

ATTITUDE CHECK

Read 1 Thessalonians 5:12-22.

"Give thanks in all circumstances, for this is God's will for you in Christ Jesus" (v. 18).

Mike Leach didn't inherit a downtrodden program as many coaches do when he took over at Texas Tech after the 1999 season. He did, however, have to change the collective attitude — about playing the smaller programs.

Leach said that one attitude he discovered in Lubbock that infuriated him was the mindset that games against someone other than the big boys such as Texas and Oklahoma weren't important, that they would be an easy win. "That attitude created this sick sort of self-fulfilling prophecy," he said.

Recent history backed him up; Tech had lost to North Texas two of the last three seasons. While the Mean Green was excited to play Tech, "the Red Raiders just acted like they were too good to play them."

That attitude revealed itself early in Leach's first season. Next up after a pair of wins was none other than North Texas. In the locker room, the head coach overheard two players discussing the upcoming game. "I'll be glad when we get on to the big games, instead of these little games that don't really count," one player said. "Yeah, I know. Tell me about it," the other player responded.

Needless to say, that attitude did not make Leach very happy. At the next team meeting, he discussed North Texas — and everyone on the schedule. And he didn't mince words. "You don't think North Texas is a big game?" he said. "Try losing to them." He then added, "If you're not excited about playing, well then you're in the wrong place, so get out of here."

Quarterback Kliff Kingsbury welcomed the chewing out. "He made a big deal that you can't take anybody lightly," he said. The result was a major attitude adjustment. The Raiders beat North Texas that Saturday, and a hallmark of the Leach era in Lubbock was that Tech did not lose the games it was supposed to win.

How's your attitude? You can fuss because your house is not as big as some, because a coworker talks too much, or because you have to take pills daily. Or you can appreciate your home for providing warmth and shelter, the co-worker for the lively conversation, and the medicine for keeping you reasonably healthy.

Whether life is endured or enjoyed depends largely on your attitude. An attitude of thankfulness to God offers you the best chance to get the most out of your life because living in gratitude means you choose joy in your life no matter what your circumstances. This world does not exist to satisfy you, so chances are it will not. True contentment and joy are found in a deep, abiding relationship with God, and the proper way to approach God is not with haughtiness or anger but with gratitude for all he has given you.

You have to have respect for everybody you play. That was a major attitude adjustment [Mike Leach] made in the program.
— *Kliff Kingsbury*

Your attitude greatly determines the quality of your life and of your relationship with God.

DAY 87

WORK ETHIC

Read Matthew 9:35-38.

"Then he said to his disciples, 'The harvest is plentiful but the workers are few. Ask the Lord of the harvest, therefore, to send out workers into his harvest field'" (vv. 37-38).

Carlos Francis worked so hard that he excelled at two sports when he was at Tech. At the same time.

Francis was a star wide receiver for the Red Raider football team from 2000-03, twice All-Big 12. When he came out of high school, few big-time programs expected him to amount to much — except for Tech. But he attacked football and worked at it just as hard as he worked at track. That's because while he was at Tech, he also was an All-Big 12 sprinter for the track team.

Francis patterned himself after the legendary pro receiver Jerry Rice, renowned for his fanatical work habits. When Francis grew tired, he simply asked himself what Rice would do. He answered his own question by getting up and working some more.

Francis also, however, turned his penchant for hard work loose on another sport, much to the chagrin of one of his fellow Tech receivers. Since NCAA rules declared that football coaches had to give their players one day off each week, Monday was in effect a football holiday at Tech.

As a sophomore in 2001, Francis looked around for something to do on his day off. After all, he couldn't just sit around. So he decided to take up golf. Inside receiver Dupree Scovell was there the day Francis first wrapped his mitts around a golf club. "It was just terrible," he said.

Naturally, though, Francis went to work on his golf game. "He wanted to get so good at it that he played it all the time," Scovell said. Francis played nearly every Monday and soon was shooting in the mid-80s. He once, though, did better than that. One Monday he made it around the course in 79. "I've been playing for 15 years," Scovell said, "and I still haven't shot 79."

It was just another result of Carlos Francis' hard work.

Do you embrace hard work or try to avoid it? No matter how hard you may try, you really can't escape hard work. Funny thing about all these labor-saving devices like cell phones and laptop computers: You're working longer and harder than ever. For many of us, our work defines us perhaps more than any other aspect of our lives. But there's a workforce you're a part of that doesn't show up in any Labor Department statistics or any IRS records.

You're part of God's staff; God has a specific job that only you can do for him. It's often referred to as a "calling," but it amounts to your serving God where there is a need in the way that best suits your God-given abilities and talents.

You should stand ready to work for God all the time, 24-7. Those are awful hours, but the benefits are out of this world.

If you need to give a guy an example on working hard, Carlos is someone you point to.
— Tech head coach Mike Leach on Carlos Francis

God calls you to work for him using the talents and gifts he gave you; whether you're a worker or a malingerer is up to you.

MIRACLE PLAY

Read Matthew 12:38-42.

"He answered, 'A wicked and adulterous generation asks for a miraculous sign!'" (v. 39)

The play was so miraculous that the Texas Tech legend who made it up in the huddle broke into tears when he pulled it off.

Donny Anderson literally rewrote the school record book. (See Devotion No. 19.) He started at halfback for three seasons (1963-65) and was also the team's punter. Often used to return kicks, he had a 100-yard kickoff return for a touchdown in the 17-14 defeat of Oklahoma State in 1965.

Anderson was so versatile that following his junior year, he was named to one All-America team as an end. His head coach, JT King, wasn't surprised and didn't mind. "After all," he said, "I recruited him to play linebacker."

Great plays were an Anderson staple, but he once managed a play that — as college football plays go — was miraculous.

The Red Raiders had beaten Kansas and been soundly whipped by Texas when they hosted the 1-1 Aggies of Texas A&M on Oct. 2, 1965. The game was hard-fought and close, but A&M had apparently saved itself and broken the Raiders' hearts with a late touchdown. The Aggies scored with 1:38 left to take the lead.

After a good kickoff return, Tech set up at its own 49. King called for a sideline pass to move the chains and stop the clock. Quarterback Tom Wilson was to pass to end Jerry Shipley, who would immediately step out of bounds. In the huddle, though, Anderson changed the play. He told Shipley, "After you catch the ball, and, if you're open, look for me because I'll be there somewhere. Pitch it to me. I think I can go."

Shipley was wide open, caught Wilson's pass, and pitched the ball to Anderson. He went the last 37 yards untouched to score with 1:18 left for the 20-16 win. He joined in the bedlam when he broke into tears after he scored the miraculous touchdown.

A late touchdown on a long pass play to pull off a comeback is termed "miraculous" because it defies defy rational explanation. Like escaping with minor abrasions from an accident that totals your car. Or recovering from an illness that seemed terminal. Underlying the notion of miracles is the idea that they are rare instances of direct divine intervention that reveal God.

But life shows us quite the contrary, that miracles are anything but rare. Since God made the world and everything in it, every-thing around you is miraculous. Even you are a miracle. Your life thus can be mundane, dull, and ordinary, or it can be spent in a glorious attitude of childlike wonder and awe. It depends on whether or not you see the world through the eyes of faith. Only through faith can you discern the hand of God in any event; only through faith can you see the miraculous and thus see God.

Jesus knew that miracles don't produce faith, but rather faith produces miracles.

I knew one thing; they weren't going to catch me after I caught the ball.
  — Donny Anderson on the miraculous play that beat Texas A&M

Miracles are all around us,
but it takes the eyes of faith to see them.

DAY 89

IMPOSSIBLE DREAM

Read Matthew 19:16-26.

"Jesus looked at them and said, 'With man this is impossible, but with God all things are possible'" (v. 26).

There was simply no way the Red Raiders could beat Oklahoma — but they did.

It wasn't that Tech was that bad the night of Oct. 22, 2011. It's just that the Sooners were that formidable. First of all, the game was in Norman where OU had won 39 straight games, the longest such streak in college football. Secondly, Oklahoma was ranked No. 1 in the coaches' poll. Texas Tech started playing football in 1925, and in all that time the program had never beaten a top-ranked team on the road. The experts gave Tech little chance; OU was an overwhelming 29-point favorite.

So the Red Raiders went out and pulled off the impossible — and there was nothing fluky or bizarre about it. The offense racked up 572 yards and scored five touchdowns in the 41-38 upset. The defense held the Sooners scoreless for eight consecutive possessions after OU scored a touchdown on its opening drive.

That scoreless streak included a missed field goal, a fumble, and six three-and-outs. By that time, Tech led 31-7 in the third quarter. Oklahoma desperately tried to save itself with two late touchdown drives, but couldn't pull off the impossible comeback.

Quarterback Seth Doege led the Red Raider offense with 441 yards through the air, four touchdowns, and no interceptions.

Wide receiver Alex Torres (See Devotion No. 2.) caught three of the scoring tosses. OU rallied to within 31-24 early in the fourth quarter, so Doege led the offense on successive scoring drives that put the game away.

"They whipped us in every part of the game," declared OU head coach Bob Stoops. "A lot of people thought we couldn't do this," Doege said. Not the Raiders; they believed they could pull off the impossible and thus wound up with "the biggest road triumph in Tech history."

Let's face it. Any pragmatic person, no matter how deep his faith may run, has to admit that we have succeeded in turning God's beautiful world into an impossible mess. The only hope for this dying, sin-infested place lies in our Lord's return to set everything right.

But we can't just give up and sit around praying for Jesus' return, as glorious a day as that will be. Our mission in this world is to change it for Jesus. We serve a Lord who calls us to step out in faith into seemingly impossible situations. We serve a Lord so audacious that he inspires us to believe that we are the instruments through which God does the impossible.

Changing the world may indeed seem impossible. Changing our little corner of it, however, is not. It is, rather, a very possible, doable act of faith.

When you go on the road and beat the No. 1 team, it is really special, almost impossible to do.
— *Tech head coach Tommy Tuberville*

With God, nothing is impossible,
including changing the world for Jesus.

DAY 90

THE GREATEST

Read Mark 9:33-37.

"If anyone wants to be first, he must be the very last, and the servant of all" (v. 35).

Sheryl Swoopes had the greatest game in the history of the NCAA Tournament championship. As a result, Texas Tech had the greatest moment in its athletic history.

On April 4, 1993, the fifth-ranked Lady Red Raiders (30-3) met third-ranked Ohio State (28-3) in Atlanta's Omni for the national championship of women's collegiate basketball. Win or lose, it would be the final game of Swoopes' incredible collegiate career.

In just two seasons (1991-93) in Lubbock, Swoopes established herself as the greatest player in Texas Tech history and one of the greatest college players ever. She was a two-time All-America and was the Naismith College Player of the Year in 1993.

She saved her greatest performance, though, for that final championship game when her team needed her most. The Raiders were the underdogs, but no matter how the Buckeyes tried, they couldn't stop Swoopes. They used five different players to guard her in their man-to-man set. They attacked her with their matchup zone and made her work for her shots.

But as Swoopes put it, "At a point in the game, I just felt I wanted to take control." And so she did. She hit a championship-game record 16 field goals to go with 11 free throws. With 13:42 to play, she smashed the women's title game record of 28 points.

With 58 seconds left, her teammates cleared out the middle of the floor and let her go to work. She hit a layup and was fouled. The subsequent free throw eclipsed Bill Walton's all-time championship-game record of 44 points. She finished up with 47 points.

That free throw also gave the Lady Raiders an 80-73 lead and wrapped up the first national title in Texas Tech's history in any sport. "It's the greatest feeling any of us have had in our athletic careers," said head coach Marsha Sharp about the championship.

Sheryl Swoopes was the greatest and so were the Lady Raiders.

We all want to be the greatest. The goal for the Red Raiders and their fans every season is at least a conference championship. The competition at work is to be the most productive sales person on the staff or the Teacher of the Year. In other words, we define being the greatest in terms of the struggle for personal success. It's nothing new; Jesus' disciples saw greatness in the same way.

As Jesus illustrated, though, greatness in the Kingdom of God has nothing to do with the secular world's understanding of success. Rather, the greatest are those who channel their ambition toward the furtherance of Christ's kingdom through love and service, rather than their own advancement. This is a complete reversal of status and values as the world sees them.

After all, who could be greater than the person who has Jesus for a brother and God for a father? And that's every one of us.

There are no words to explain how great a player Sheryl Swoopes is.
— Marsha Sharp

To be great for God has nothing to do
with personal advancement and everything to do
with the advancement of Christ's kingdom.

LESSON LEARNED

Read Psalm 143.

"Teach me to do your will, for you are my God" (v. 10).

Being fired from his first job taught Spike Dykes a lesson that served him well the rest of his coaching career.

Dykes was 21 and "green as a gourd" in 1959 when he landed his first job for $3,280 a year. For that princely sum, he was an assistant football coach and the head basketball, tennis, and golf coach. He taught five classes daily, all different subjects. So how did he do? He was fired "almost immediately."

On a bus ride home after a losing basketball game, Dykes took offense to the nonchalant way his kids took the defeat as they laughed and tossed their sandwich bags around. Finally, he announced that the next guy throwing stuff would himself be thrown off the bus. Dykes later admitted, "It was stupid to draw a line in the sand over a little flying baloney."

Sure enough, a sack sailed right at him. "If the kid had been as good a shot with the basketball as he was with the bag, we might have won the game," the disgruntled coach said. Backed into a corner, Dykes had no choice but to put the kid off the bus, which happened to be several miles from the school.

About three a.m., the coach got a call from the superintendent who wasted no time. He was fired. "Twenty-one years old, about to become a father, and I was fired from my first coaching job," Dykes recalled. And he was tickled about it. "That job was so bad that getting fired felt like getting paroled," he said. His boss insisted, however, that he finish out the school year.

And the valuable lesson the future Texas Tech head football coach learned from the whole deal? "There's a lot worse things that can happen to you" than getting fired. Dykes realized that instability and change were part of the coaching profession.

Learning about anything in life requires a combination of education and experience. Education is the accumulation of facts that we call knowledge; experience is the acquisition of wisdom and discernment, which add purpose and understanding to our knowledge. Education without experience just doesn't have much practical value in our world today.

The most difficult way to learn is trial and error: just dive in blindly and mess up. Better luck next time. The best way to learn is through example coupled with a set of instructions. With this process, someone has gone ahead to show you the way and has written down all the information you need to follow.

In teaching us the way to live godly lives, God chose the latter method. He set down in his book the habits, actions, and attitudes that make for a way of life in accordance with his wishes. He also sent us Jesus to explain and to illustrate.

God teaches us not only how to exist but how to live. We just need to be attentive students.

I was never afraid about keeping a job after that, or worried too much about what was going to happen.
– Spike Dykes on the lesson he learned from being fired from his first job

To learn from Jesus is to learn what life is all about and how God means for us to live it.

THE FINISH LINE

Read 2 Timothy 4:1-8.

"I have fought the good fight, I have finished the race, I have kept the faith" (v. 7).

In football, it's not always how you start. Sometimes it's how you finish. Just ask Kansas after the 2013 encounter with Tech.

The Red Raiders of 2013 would win eight games and defeat Arizona State in the Holiday Bowl. On Oct. 5, though, against a team that had lost 21 conference games in a row, 20th-ranked Tech looked like the underdog early on. Kansas quickly put a touchdown and a field goal on the scoreboard.

Meanwhile, the Red Raiders practically sleepwalked through four possessions. An interception led to the KU field goal, and busted coverage on a pass play resulted in the touchdown. On offense, the Raiders flubbed a field-goal try.

Thus, the first quarter ended with KU leading 10-0, a state of affairs that was to change in a hurry. Tech head coach Kliff Kingsbury said that in the second quarter, "Our offense did a good job not panicking, continued just to make routine plays, and things started kind of snowballing for us."

Snowballing indeed — to the tune of 54 straight points.

The fast finish started early in the second quarter when Ryan Bustin kicked the first of his four field goals. Kenny Williams scored from the 1 with 7:46 left in the half to tie the game. Wide receiver Shawn Corker pulled off a big defensive play by stuffing a fake punt that gave Tech the ball at the Kansas 16. Quarterback Baker Mayfield ran it in from there, and the rout was on.

Tech led 20-10 at the half, having scored all 20 points in the final twelve minutes. The count was 37-10 after three quarters and went to 54-10 before the Jayhawks managed a meaningless score. With a blazing finish after a slow start, Tech won 54-16.

Paul uses a sports metaphor in comparing the faith life of the Christian to a race. His point is not that we are to drive ourselves to the point of exhaustion as runners often do, but rather that the most important part of our faith journey is the finish line.

Our lives will end; each of us will cross that finish line in one way or another. One of sports' most inspiring sights is that of a runner who falls down but nevertheless gets back up and finishes the race. Our faith lives must be like that.

That's because as we attempt to journey through life faithfully, we will stumble and fall down, metaphorically at least. In the personal race each of us runs, we will be tested, we will face hardships, we will be scorned and ridiculed, we will be called upon to make sacrifices, we will see our testimony rejected.

But for the disciple of Jesus Christ, these are merely hurdles, not barriers. Our task is to keep the faith; we keep running. When it's all over and the race has been run, each of us is the final arbiter of whether we finish the race in glory or in defeat.

Getting started is the hardest part. But when we get in a groove and get things going, then we're on a roll.
    — Tech wide receiver Eric Ward after the 2013 Kansas game

**We win the race that is our lives
by keeping the faith.**

DOWNRIGHT CRAZY

Read Luke 13:31-35.

"Some Pharisees came to Jesus and said to him, 'Leave this place and go somewhere else. Herod wants to kill you.' He replied, 'Go tell that fox . . . I must keep going today and tomorrow and the next day'" (vv. 31-33).

The Texas Tech fans didn't behave at all. *Sports Illustrated* said they "acted as crazed as ranch hands who have been out in the West Texas heat too long." They had good reason to go nuts.

On Oct. 30, 1976, the local and area residents went bonkers for the Red Raiders. They packed Jones Stadium — even to the tune of paying seven dollars to stand up — for a game against Texas "that very nearly sent both coaching staffs and every one of the 54,187 spectators . . . to the rubber room." The undefeated, sixth-ranked Raiders teamed with the Longhorns to stage a classic.

Like the fans, head coach Steve Sloan's second team had some zany aspects to it. Starting quarterback Rodney Allison, for instance, declared the day before the game, "I don't feel I'm a first-class passer." Then he went out and drilled the Longhorns with 10-of-11 passing for 87 yards and scored on a 5-yard run.

Perhaps the most unusual aspect of the team was placekicker Brian Hall, who kicked with an artificial leg. "As long as there is glue, I'll never have shin splints," he said. He noted that any cold weather engendered by six inches of West Texas snow on Friday wouldn't hurt his toes one bit. His second-quarter field goal ultimately proved to be the difference in the wild 31-28 win that saw the Red Raiders come from behind twice on their way to a 10-1 season.

Billy Taylor scored Tech's first and last touchdowns, both from the 1, with strong safety Larry Dupre's interception setting up the initial score. Larry Isaac had a 15-yard TD run on his way to 91 yards for the day, which let him break Donny Anderson's Tech career rushing record.

"We've got something here that's exciting," declared defensive end Harold Buell. And, for the fans, more than a little crazy

What some see as crazy often is shrewd instead. Like the time you went into business for yourself or when you decided to go back to school. Maybe it was when you fixed up that old house. Or when you bought that new company's stock.

You know a good thing when you see it but are also shrewd enough to spot something that's downright crazy. Jesus was that way too. He knew that his entering Jerusalem was in complete defiance of all apparent reason and logic since a whole bunch of folks who wanted to kill him were waiting for him there.

Nevertheless, he went because he also knew that when the great drama had played out he would defeat not only his personal enemies but the most fearsome enemy of all: death itself.

It was, after all, a shrewd move that provided the way to your salvation.

Lubbock's lunacy hit a new bonkers level.
— SI's Ron Reid on the reaction to the win over Texas

It's so good it sounds crazy — but it's not: through faith in Jesus, you can have eternal life with God.

DAY 94

TURNAROUND

Read Acts 9:1-22.

*"All those who heard him were astonished and asked,
'Isn't he the man who raised havoc in Jerusalem among
those who call on this name?'" (v. 21)*

The Red Raiders were getting embarrassed right in front of the home folks until they pulled off the biggest turnaround in school history to that point.

"I wasn't happy," said Tech head coach Mike Leach about the carnage he was watching on Sept. 25, 2004. Inflicting the damage were the TCU Horned Frogs. In their first visit to Lubbock since 1995, they jumped out to a 21-0 lead in the second quarter. Looking for some way to turn this thing around, Leach called a time out. He had something to say and he said it quite forcefully.

Senior All-American wide receiver Trey Haverty was on the field that day. He was named the Red Raiders' safeties coach in 2013. In 2015, he took over the outside linebackers before becoming the defensive coordinator at Lamar in 2016. He recalled that during the timeout Leach "gave us some profound words."

Senior linebacker Mike Smith, a four-year starter whose pro career was cut short by a shoulder injury, was likewise present for Leach's chosen words. Smith joined the Tech coaching staff in 2013. In 2015, he was named the co-defensive coordinator and coach of the defensive line. His memory of the time out was a little more blunt than was Haverty's. "Leach called us [over] and cursed at us about a hundred times," he said.

Both players agreed that the time out helped the team begin a memorable turnaround. After not scoring on their first seven possessions, the Red Raiders rolled up 70 points on the way to a 70-35 rout. "We knew it would snowball once it started," said senior quarterback Sonny Cumbie, who threw for 441 yards.

Like the Red Raiders against TCU in 2004, we often look for some means or some spark we can use to turn our lives around. Oh, we may not be headed to prison, be bankrupt, or be tormented by an addiction. Maybe we can't find a purpose to our life and are just drifting.

Still, our situation often seems untenable to us. We sink into gloom and despair, wasting our time, our emotions, and our energy by fretting about how bad things are and how they will never get better. How in the world can we turn things around?

Turn to Jesus; as the old hymn urges, trust and obey him. If it's that simple, then why hesitate? Well, it's also that complicated as Paul discovered when he experienced one of the most dramatic turnarounds in history. To surrender to Jesus is to wind up with a new life, and to wind up with a new life, we have to surrender to Jesus. We have to give up control.

What's to lose? After all, if we're looking for a way to turn our lives around, we're not doing such a good job of running things. What's to gain? A better life here and an eternal life with God.

We had a little run and put up some points and won the game.
— Trey Haverty's understated description of the 2004 TCU game

**A life in need of turning around
needs Jesus at the wheel.**

DAY 95

THE END

Read Revelation 22:1-17.

"I am the Alpha and the Omega, the First and the Last, the Beginning and the End" (v. 13).

The first great era in Texas Tech football came to a sudden and surprising end, precipitated by a dispute over what amounted to a bowl game.

From 1930-40, Pete Cawthon led the Matadors/Red Raiders to 76 wins and their first two bowl games. The 1940 season with its 9-1-1 record was one of his best. The team took on opponents from all over the country, including Loyola University of Los Angeles, Montana, Brigham Young, Marquette (Milwaukee), Miami, Centenary (Louisiana), Wake Forest, St. Louis, New Mexico, and San Francisco University. That was part of the problem.

For some time, the Tech athletic council had been upset with the head coach's refusal to schedule more than a handful of Texas teams. Over the last six seasons, Tech had played only seven Texas schools, including none in 1940. The proposed 1941 schedule also lacked a single state opponent. Cawthon wouldn't play smaller Texas teams, and the big-time state programs wouldn't play Tech because they had nothing to gain and had a good chance of losing.

Following the 23-21 win over San Francisco that ended the 1940 season, Cawthon and his players came home from the coast to find the homefolks stirred up about a game with undefeated Hardin-Simmons. Cawthon and assistant Dutchey Smith bitterly opposed the proposed contest and let everyone know about it. In a secret ballot, the Tech players voted 33-3 against the game.

Tech's president asked Cawthon if he would be interested in his team playing in a bowl game or a game against a "big name" from the Southwest Conference. Cawthon said he would, but he again shot down the idea of playing Hardin-Simmons.

Displeased, the athletic council asked for Cawthon's resignation; he tendered it, they accepted it. The Cawthon era had ended.

Pete Cawthon's tenure as Tech's head football coach is another example of one of life's basic truths: Everything ends. Even the stars have a life cycle, though admittedly it's rather lengthy. Erosion eventually will wear a boulder to a pebble. Life itself is temporary; all living things have a beginning and an end.

Within the framework of our own lifetimes, we experience endings. Loved ones, friends, and pets die; relationships fracture; jobs dry up; our health, clothes, lawn mowers, TV sets — they all wear out. Even this world as we know it will end.

But one of the greatest ironies of God's gift of life is that not even death is immune from the great truth of creation that all things must end. That's because through Jesus' life, death, and resurrection, God himself acted to end any power death once had over life. In other words, because of Jesus, the end of life has ended. Eternity is ours for the claiming.

When Cawthon submitted his resignation, it was truly the end of an era in Texas Tech football.
— Ralph Sellmeyer and James Davidson in The Red Raiders

Everything ends;
thanks to Jesus Christ, so does death.

NOTES
(by Devotion Day Number)

1   In February 1923, the state . . . held on Sept. 15, 1925,: Ralph L. Sellmeyer and James E. Davidson, *The Red Raiders* (Huntsville, Ala.: The Strode Publishers, Inc., 1978), p. 11.

1   Texas Tech formally opened . . . coach effective July 1, 1925.: Sellmeyer and Davidson, p. 12.

1   Grady Higginbotham, who had played . . . only a one-column shot.: Sellmeyer and Davidson, p. 14.

1   that first team consisted mostly of . . . of varsity college football.: Sellmeyer and Davidson, p. 20.

1   Captain Winfeld "Windy" Nicklaus was . . . major-college freshman ball.: Sellmeyer and Davidson, p. 18.

1   this "Rag Tail Bunch": Sellmeyer and Davidson, p. 17.

1   They had no tradition . . . know quite what to expect.: Sellmeyer and Davidson, p. 20.

2   Torres first made his . . . what we expect around here.": Chris Mahr, "Putting His Career in Flight," *Sports Illustrated*, Aug. 12, 2011, http://sportsillustrated.cnn.com/vault/article/magazine/MAG1188661/index.htm.

2   [The younger wideouts] call me . . . warm up than they do.: Mahr, "Putting His Career in Flight."

3   Texas Tech assistant Pat . . . for at least two years.: Jay Posner, "Captain Gave Raiders Berth in Sweet Sixteen." *The San Diego Union-Tribune*, March 22, 2005, htttp://www.utsandiego.com/uniontrib/20050322/news_1s22ncaa.html.

3   Oklahoma's head coach said . . . his ability to get open.: Posner, "Captain Gives Raiders Berth."

3   an "all-court masterpiece": Kelli Anderson, "Tech Knockout," *Sports Illustrated*, March 28, 2005, http://sportsillustrated.cnn.com/vault/article/magazine/MAG1110341/index.htm.

3   "I have never had a player I've had more admiration for.": Anderson, "Tech Knockout."

3   A lot of people doubted . . . wrong is a good thing.: Anderson, "Tech Knockout."

4   "a cowboy who just happened to play football,": Ray Westbrook, "E.J. Holub Is Famous," *Lubbock Avalanche-Journal*, Feb. 20, 2013, http://lubbockonline.com/life-columnists/2013-02-10.

4   Asked once how long . . . coming in for a visit.": Westbrook, "E.J. Holub Is Famous."

4   [Mike] Ditka kept riding . . . horse and went in there.: Westbrook, "E.J. Holub Is Famous."

5   "I thought I would still . . . couldn't have dreamt of it.": Ivan Maisel, "The Good Life of Kliff Kingsbury," *ESPN.com*, July 4, 2013, http://espn.go.com/college-football/story/_/id9447111.

5   the last few days had been -- beyond ecstatic to be back,": Don Williams, "Texas Tech Names Kingsbury New Head Coach," *Lubbock Avalanche-Journal*, Dec. 13, 2012, http://lubbockonline.com/filed-online/2012-12-12.

5   "I loved it out here," . . . thrilled to be back.": Don Williams, "Texas Tech Names Kingsbury."

5   "I think it's a great day for Texas Tech,": Don Williams, "Texas Tech Names Kingsbury."

5   He said he always wanted to be back ever since: Don Williams, "Texas Tech Names Kingsbury."

5   Let me tell you. It's good to be home.: Michael DuPont II, "Kingsbury Welcomed as New Head Coach," *The Daily Toreador*, Dec. 14, 2012, http://www.dailytoreador.com/news/article_1bd6becc-4626-11e2-8d4a-0019bb30f31a.html.

6   He had broken his leg . . . counted on him for 1944.: Sellmeyer and Davidson, p. 150.

6   The *Lubbock Avalanche-Journal* . . . rushed for 123 yards.: Sellmeyer and Davidson, p. 153.

6   he didn't come into the game . . . second score in the fourth quarter: Sellmeyer and Davidson, p. 157.

6   The latter two were . . . didn't play a major schedule.: Sellmeyer and Davidson, p. 160.

6   I am disappointed about Schlinkman.: Sellmeyer and Davidson, p. 160.

7   On April 4, 1993, a reporter . . . to celebrate with the students.": Patrick Gonzales, "Looking Back: Lady Raiders Win National Championship," *Texas Tech Today*, Feb. 17, 2013, http://today.ttu.edu/2013/02/looking-back.

7   When the players stepped . . . home at Jones Stadium.: Linda Carriger, "A Legendary Red Raider: Sheryl Swoopes," in *Raiding the SWC*, Gina Augustini, Kent Best, and Darrel Thomas, eds. (Lubbock: Texas Tech Student Publications, 1996), p. 124.

7   We basically missed the best party ever on campus.: Patrick Gonzales, "Looking Back."

8   The sophomore quarterback stood . . . go score a touchdown.: Terry Greenberg, "Harrell Quiets Raucous Kyle Field," in "Don Williams' 10 Memorable Moments of the Texas Tech-A&M Rivalry," *RedRaiders.com*, Oct. 7, 2011, http://redraiders.com/sports-red-raiders-football/2011-10-07.

8   When A&M blitzed, Harrell . . . crazy to absolutely silent.": Greenberg, "Harrell Quiets Raucous Kyle Field."

8   He would tell me the first play and usually say something motivational.: Greenberg, "Harrell Quiets Raucous Kyle Field."

9   Dykes said it took a couple . . .supposed to do that.": Spike Dykes with Dave Boling, *Spike Dykes's Tales from the Texas Tech Sideline* (Champaign, Ill.: Sports Publishing L.L.C., 2004), p. 3.

9   Dykes assumed he had . . . each other in high school,: Dykes with Boling, *Spike Dykes's Tales*, p. 3.

9   McWilliams told all ten . . . to join him in Austin.: Dykes with Boling, *Spike Dykes's Tales*, p. 3.

9   About an hour after McWilliams resigned,: Dykes with Boling, *Spike Dykes's Tales*, p. 6.

9   There was no doubt . . . that's what we needed.: Dykes with Boling, *Spike Dykes's Tales*, p. 6.

10   after being refused in 1927, 1929, 1931, and 1952,: Sellmeyer and Davidson, p. 226.

10   "caused the biggest celebration . . . end of World War II.": Sellmeyer and Davidson, p. 225.

10   "a personal triumph" for DeWitt Weaver: Sellmeyer and Davidson, p. 226.

10   In 1952, Tech officials thought . . . of my stay at Tech,": Sellmeyer and Davidson, p. 228.

10   The Border Conference, of which . . . to get a good night's sleep.: Sellmeyer and Davidson, p. 231.

10   It had started with a wish . . . hind legs in the '50s.: Sellmeyer and Davidson, p. 232.

11   In just a few years, . . . it into a powerhouse.": Rodger Sherman, "How Chris Beard Built Texas Tech," *TheRinger.com*, April 3, 2019, https://www.theringer.com/march-madness/2019/4/3/18293467/chris-beard-texas-tech-jarrett-culver-final-four-defense.

11   "the best defense in . . . title because of it.": Sherman, "How Christ Beard Built Texas Tech."

11   The basketball team has instituted a revolutionary defensive scheme.: Sherman, "How Christ Beard Built Texas Tech."

12   "I think we schemed them . . . down their big receivers,": Jose Rodriquez, "Tech D Proves Worth," *The Daily Toreador*, Oct. 15, 2012, http://www.dailytoreador.com/sports/article_0d04b184-168c-11e2-9d17-001a4bcf6878.html.

12   Defensive tackle Kerry Hyder . . . the pocket several times.: Rodriguez, "Tech D Proves Worth."

12   We kind of fell off last week and kind of took it personal.: Michael DuPont II, "Red Raiders Dominate Mountaineers," *The Daily Toreador*, Oct. 15, 2012, http://www.dailytoreador.com/sports/article_26bded1c-15b4-11e2-a3f7-001a4bcf6878.html.

13   Tech head coach JT King . . . carry his senior season.: Sellmeyer and Davidson, p. 340.

13   "was the fastest guy . . . on one-on-one coverage.": Don Williams, "Claude Grad, Tech All-American Denton Fox Dies," *Amarillo Globe-News*, April 30, 2013, http://amarillo.com/news/local-news/2013-04-30.

13   "He had a way of being in the right place at the right time,": Sellmeyer and Davidson, p. 341.

13   "Denton was one of . . . up when you needed him.": Sellmeyer and Davidson, p. 342.

13   Much of the 1963 movie . . . teenaged extras in the film.: Don Williams, "Claude Grad."

13   [Denton] and [his wife] Sara . . . were two of those.: Don Williams, "Claude Grad."

14   In the spring of 1984, . . . where I wanted to be.": JT Leeson, "A Texas Tech Legend," *TexasTech.com*, Oct. 12, 2001, http://www.texastech.com/sports/m-footbl/spec-rel/101201aaa.html.

14   One night at bed . . . in the crowded city.: Dykes with Boling, *Spike Dykes's Tales*, p. 37.

14   "We all had some troubles . . . what time it was.: Dykes with Boling, *Spike Dykes's Tales*, p. 37.

14   Hey, he was out there getting exercise.": Dykes with Boling, *Spike Dykes's Tales*, p. 38.

14   Heck, we weren't sure what DAY it was.: Dykes with Boling, *Spike Dykes's Tales*, p. 37.

15   The subject of the . . . with in-line skating.: Don Williams, "Broken Arm Won't Keep Tech's Leach Off Sidelines," *Lubbock Avalance-Journal*, Oct. 9, 2007, http://lubbockonline.com/stories/100907/col_100907012.shtml.

15   Just after he moved to . . . to start his new hobby: Michael Lewis, "Coach Leach Goes Deep, Very Deep," *The New York Times*, Dec. 4, 2005, http://www.nytimes.com/2005/12/04/magazine/04coach.html.

15   "I've never gotten injured . . . palms of both hands." Williams, "Broken Arm."

15   It's a mess. . . . It's a nuisance.: Williams, "Broken Arm."

16   Adams drew interest from . . .the place I needed to go.": Chois Woodman, "Luke Adams: Not the Typical Division I Basketball Player," *The Daily Toreador*, Feb. 13, 2012, http://www.dailytoreador.com/sports/article_e35c7e9c-56bb-11e1-b128-001a4bcf6878.html.

16   "When I grew up, . . . sorry for myself either.": Woodman, "Luke Adams."

16   Adams has a cochlear . . . never let that affect him.": Woodman, "Luke Adams."

16   I like the challenge.: Woodman, "Luke Adams."

17   Oklahoma didn't want him, . . . if he couldn't get a scholarship.: Mike Leach with Bruce Feldman, *Swing Your Sword* (New York City, Diversion Books, 2012), p. 116.

17   "I'll be here as soon . . . was off the scale.": Leach with Feldman, *Swing Your Sword*, p. 117.

17   "Oh my gosh, who is this little frat guy?": Leach with Feldman, *Swing Your Sword*, p. 117.

17   "This guy is our best player.": Leach with Feldman, *Swing Your Sword*, p. 118.

17   Welker's "last-minute signing proved to be a bonanza": "Wes Welker," *Wikipedia, the free encyclopedia*, http://en.wikipedia.org/wiki/Wes_Welker.

17   Wes Welker is one of the . . . suit up for Texas Tech.: Rana L. Cash, " Texas Tech Investigates Wes Welker Tweets," *Sporting News*, June 12, 2013, http://

	www.sportingnews.com/ncaa-football/story/2013-06-12.
18	"scruffy walk-on Avery Benson.": "Louisville Becomes Latest No. 1 to Lose," *SI.com*, Dec. 11, 2019, https://www.si.com/college/college-basketball/game/2164434.
18	"highlight-reel blocks . . . teammates form the tip.": "Louisville Becomes Latest No. 1 to Lose."
18	Sometimes, it's hard to . . . be rolling at all.: "Louisville Becomes Latest No. 1 to Lose."
19	"Donny Anderson put Tech on the map.": Beilue, Jon Mark, "'The Best College Football Player in America,'" *Amarillo Globe-News*, Dec. 26, 1999, http://amarillo.com/stories/122699/spo_170-7178.shtml.
19	Anderson's time as an . . . a few more times.": Beilue, "The Best College Football Player."
19	His achievements helped change . . . kid on the block.: Beilue, "The Best College Football Player."
19	Until [his injury], the . . . of a finesse player.: Beilue, "The Best College Football Player."
20	Her dad, Charles, introduced . . . just loved [basketball] ever since.": Michael Suniga, "Morris Saddened to Leave," *The Daily Toreador*, March 7, 2013, http://www.dailytoreador.com/sports/article_aa00f750-87a6-a02d-001a4bcf6878.html.
20	her mother's alma mater. . . . family whenever she wanted.: Suniga, "Morris Saddened to Leave."
20	She just didn't fit in, . . . "They were just loyal,": Suniga, "Morris Saddened to Leave."
20	declaring she had never . . . with such a close bond.: Suniga, "Morris Saddened to Leave."
20	I feel like we are all family. We are all sisters.: Suniga, "Morris Saddened to Leave."
21	In practice the week of . . . which cut his face." Don Williams, "Don Williams' 10 Memorable Moments of the Texas Tech-A&M Rivalry," *RedRaiders.com*, Oct. 7, 2011, http://redraiders.com/sports/-red-raiders-football/2011-10-07.
21	An injury sidelined the . . . moved Morris from fullback.: Don Williams, "Don Williams' 10."
21	"We thought he could . . . tackles, and he did,": Don Williams, "Don Williams' 10."
21	[Sammy] Morris made sure to torture A&M both seasons.: Don Williams, "Don Williams' 10."
22	We came out and executed well early and it just snowballed from there.: Randy Rosetta, "Williams, Tech Bury Bears," *Lubbock Avalanche-Journal*, Oct. 28, 2001, http://lubbockonline.com/stories/102801/col_1028010013.shtml.
23	"It doesn't matter how long . . . we're going to finish it.'": Adam Zuvanich, "Tech Defense Gets Last Word in Overtime," *Lubbock Avalanche-Journal*, Oct. 12, 2008, http://lubbockonline.com/stories/101208/spo_343082509.shtml.
23	McKinner Dixon pressured the Husker. . . mobbed by his teammates,: Zuvanich, "Tech Defense Gets Last Word."
23	You're always going to be . . . do it from there.: Zuvanich, "Tech Defense Gets Last Word."
24	In the outdoor regional meet, . . . one of his fastest 700 meters.: Patrick Gonzales, "Runner Finds Inspiration under Tutelage of Tech Coach," *Lubbock Avalanche-Journal*, May 25, 2007, http://lubbockonline.com/stories/052507/col_052507084.shtml.
24	My confidence was down, . . . do this anymore.: Gonzales, "Runner Finds Inspiration."
25	"a celebration of Arizona State." . . . "It should have been.": Don Williams, "Tech Upsets No. 16 Sun Devils," *Lubbock Avalanche-Journal*, Dec. 31, 2013, http://lubbockonline.com/filed-online/2013-12-31/tech-upsets-no-14[sic]-sun-devils-37-23-win-holiday-bowl#.Vd9RQ_lViko.
25	Some pundits said they'd . . . to fuel the fire.": Bernie Wilson, "Webb's 4 TD Passes Tie Holiday Bowl Record," *Lubbock Avalanche-Journal*, Dec. 31, 2013, http://lubbockonline.com/filed-online/2013-12-31/webbs--4-td-passes-tie-holiday-bowl-record#.Vd9QGvlViko.
25	"They were the more . . . They came to play.": Wilson, "Webb's 4 TD Passes Tie Holiday Bowl."
25	We didn't get any respect all weekend long.: Wilson, ""Webb's 4 TD Passes Tie Holiday Bowl."
26	OU players and fans celebrated . . . would remind us of OU.": "Raiders Get Their Turn to Celebrate," *Lubbock Avalanche-Journal*, Nov. 22, 2009. http://lubbockonline.com/stories/112209/spo_527631907.shtml.
26	"They just kicked our butts. That's all you can say.": Courtney Linehan, "Start to Finish," *Lubbock Avalanche-Journal*, Nov. 22, 2009, http://lubbockonline.com/stories/112208/spo_527630721.shtml.
26	early in the fourth quarter, . . . [and] hopped around.": "Raiders Get Their Turn to Celebrate."
26	I was too self-conscious to dance, really.: "Raiders Get Their Turn to Celebrate."
27	" a sympathetic, God-fearing . . . respect of 'his boys.'": Sellmeyer and Davidson, p. 48.
27	he was known "to hibernate . . . for a two-hour practice.: Sellmeyer and Davidson, p. 49.
27	He sat on a medicine box . . . fall had killed him.: Sellmeyer and Davidson, p. 51.
27	We all thought he had . . . see if he was all right.: Sellmeyer and Davidson, p. 51.
28	"the best leader I've ever been around,": Max Hengst, "Brooks Steps up as Leader," *dailytoreador.com*, Oct. 9, 2019, http://www.dailytoreador.com/sports/brooks-steps-up-as-leader-star-player-for-tech-s/article_358f01126.
28	Keith Patterson said Brooks . . . good and bad.": Hengst, "Brooks Steps up as Leader."

28 "is just something I like to take pride in." Hengst, "Brooks Steps up as Leader."

28 "ambivalent, vacillating, impulsive, unsubmissive." John MacArthur, *Twelve Ordinary Men* (Nashville: W Publishing Group, 2002), p. 39.

28 "the greatest preacher" and the "dominant figure": MacArthur, *Twelve Ordinary Men*, p. 39.

29 "I was never worried because our offense was just hurting ourselves,": Don Williams, "Raiders Outgun Mississippi," *Lubbock Avalanche-Journal*, Sept. 28, 2003, http://lubbockonline.com/stories/092803/col_092803011.shtml.

29 We made some mistakes but I'm proud of the way we overcame them.: Steven Griffin, "Miscues, Turnovers Almost Ruin Big Day," *Lubbock Avalanche-Journal*, Sept. 28, 2003, http://lubbock online.com/stories/092803/col_092803012.shtml.

30 During the offseason, . . . certainly constituted an upgrade.: Dykes with Boling, p. 9.

30 "All he did," Dykes said, "was play one of the most phenomenal games.": Dykes with Boling, p. 10.

30 We needed to develop . . . anywhere at any time.: Dykes with Boling, p. 10.

31 He was credited officially . . . asserting it is too low.: Emily Elsen, "A Legendary Red Raider: Darvin Ham Served Up a Shattering Ham Slam," in *Raiding the SWC*, p. 106.

31 Sasser missed a hook shot.: Elsen, "A Legendary Red Raider: Darvin Ham," p. 106.

31 no one had ever before . . . his top-10 all-time,: Elsen, "A Legendary Red Raider: Darvin Ham," p. 106.

31 It was just an ordinary dunk with extra power.: Elsen, "A Legendary Red Raider: Darvin Ham," p. 106.

32 Head coach Dell Morgan resigned . . . to play, which was done.: Sellmeyer and Davidson, p. 188.

32 After a number of . . . to come for an interview.: Sellmeyer and Davidson, p. 191.

32 As he prepared his team . . . was born the Masked Rider.: Sellmeyer and Davidson, p. 208.

32 "the largest single event in the history of Tech football.": Sellmeyer and Davidson, p. 224.

32 It was an accomplishment . . . part of Tech football history.: Sellmeyer and Davidson, p. 192.

33 "We had some miscommunications on the field early,": Jose Rodriguez, "Red Raiders Upset No. 14 Missouri Tigers," *The Daily Toreador*, Nov. 7, 2010, http://www.dailytoreador.com/sports/article_fcb72900-ead3-11df-9229-00127992bc8b.html.

33 "I thought the coaches . . . first couple of drives,": Rodriguez, "Red Raiders Upset No. 14."

34 "I guess I was kind . . . we visited other campuses.": Sam Scott, "Hardaway Relates Tech Experience," *Lubbock Avalanche-Journal*, Feb. 7, 1999, http://lubbockonline.com/stories/020799/0207990053.shtml.

34 "I'll be a Red Raider until I die.": Scott, "Hardaway Relates Tech Experience."

34 There's a lot of people . . . thing I'm proud of.: Scott, "Hardaway Relates Tech Experience."

35 knew early on she wanted to be a Lady Raider.: Tommy Magelssen, "1993 Team Came Mostly from West Texas," *Lubbock Avalanche-Journal*, Feb. 16, 2013, http://lubbockonline.com/sports-red-raiders-womens-basketball/2013-02-15.

35 She didn't want to be that far from her family.: Magelssen, "1993 Team Came Mostly from West Texas."

35 despite her boyfriend's wish to go elsewhere.: Magelssen, "1993 Team Came Mostly from West Texas."

35 She was torn between . . . It was Lubbock Street.: Magelssen, "1993 Team Came Mostly from West Texas."

35 I prayed for a sign and looked up and saw that sign.: Magelssen, "1993 Team Came Mostly from West Texas."

36 For Red Raider strength and . . . Bam! Bam! Bam! — and screaming,": Lewis, "Coach Leach Goes Deep, Very Deep."

36 If I hadn't been there, he might have taken a swing at Mike.: Lewis, "Coach Leach Goes Deep."

37 The game was played at . . . keep out non-paying customers.": Sellmeyer and Davidson, p. 17.

37 A good crowd estimated at . . . outgained the Indians 229-96.: Sellmeyer and Davidson, p. 20.

37 Finally, with only a few seconds . . . before time had run out.: Sellmeyer and Davidson, p. 22.

37 he was convinced the Matadors . . . the call out of revenge.: Sellmeyer and Davidson, p. 22.

37 [Tech's] first game would create . . . by Matador fans and players.: Sellmeyer and Davidson, p. 20.

38 "steamed about the play . . . receivers in the game.": "Lighthearted Linemen Contrast Leach's Harsh Remarks," *Lubbock Avalanche-Journal*, Sept. 16, 2008, http://lubbockonline.com/stories/091608/spo_332866621.shtml.

38 he "offered to push . . . but that's all right,": "Lighthearted Linemen Contrast."

38 I just remember the jog to the end zone was tiring.: "Lighthearted Linemen Contrast."

39 Less than 24 hours after . . . it got real quiet,": Randy Rosetta, "Tech Players Get Taste of Knight Life," *Lubbock Avalanche-Journal*, March 25, 2001, http://lubbockonline.com/stories/032501/col_032501022.shtml.

39 Even before he visited . . . his interest in the Tech job.: Randy Rosetta, "Knight

'Livid' Over Tech Situation," *Lubbock Avalanche-Journal*, March 11, 2001, http://lubbockonline. com/stories/031101/spo_031101114.shtml.

39   "He told us the way . . . and go to class.": Rosetta, "Tech Players Get Taste of Knight Life."

39   He let us know . . . we've ever been through.: Rosetta, "Tech Players Get Taste of Knight Life."

40   Rounding out the north end . . . between the two sides.: Sellmeyer and Davidson, p. 252.

40   moving more than six . . . concrete and steel 200 feet.: Sellmeyer and Davidson, p. 251.

40   The firm chosen for the . . . took only a few days.: Sellmeyer and Davidson, p. 253.

40   The amazing part fascinated . . . watched with open mouths.: Sellmeyer and Davidson, p. 253.

41   "They had struggled . . . going to run the ball," Tommy Magelssen, "Tech Upends UH 35-20," *The Daily Toreador*, Nov. 28, 2010, http://www.dailytoreador.com/sports/article_f099558a-fb5e-11df-8cd1-00127992bc8b.html.

41   All game long Houston . . . the last few weeks.": Magelssen, "Tech Upends UH 35-20."

41   I just basically quit . . . have done it earlier.: Magelssen, "Tech Upends UH 35-20."

42   He changed "the image of . . . renown in the process.": Sellmeyer and Davidson, p. 46.

42   Cawthon fashioned himself . . . the evening sobbing violently.: Sellmeyer and Davidson, p. 48.

42   on a plane trip home after . . . wants to die like him.": Sellmeyer and Davidson, pp. 50-51.

42   Cawthon told his team one . . . ain't no such word.": Sellmeyer and Davidson, p. 47.

42   On the first day of practice . . . head coach walked away.: Sellmeyer and Davidson, p. 46.

42   You know what? I was convinced.: Sellmeyer and Davidson, p. 46.

43   "It's hard,": George Watson, "Fuller Trades Pads for Glove," *Lubbock Avalanche-Journal*, Jan. 14, 2004, http://lubbockonline.com/stories/011404/col_011404017.shtml.

43   "The only thing that . . . to play in a baseball game.: "Cody Fuller," *ZoomInfo.com*, http://www. zoominfo.com/p/Cody-Fuller/86115961.

43   "Playing two sports can . . . was missed in baseball.": Watson, "Fuller Trades Pads for Glove."

43   I think you've got to love this game.: "Cody Fuller," *ZoomInfo.com*.

44   I didn't see anybody on our sideline that didn't think we could win.": Don Williams, "Barnburner on the Brazos," *Lubbock Avalanche-Journal*, Oct. 6, 2002, http://lubbockonline.com/stories/100602/col_1006020018.shtml.

44   "At that point, maybe . . . sensed something brewing.: Williams, "Barnburner on the Brazos."

44   Wes Welker was cramping up . . . wanted to go in.: Brent Schrotenboer, "Raiders' Magic Comes Back to Haunt Aggies," *Lubbock Avalanche-Journal*, Oct. 6, 2002, http://lubbockonline.com/stories/100602/col_1006020016.shtml.

44   I think everybody believes in this offense.: Williams, "Barnburner on the Brazos."

45   during the summer of . . . our minds ready to play.": Don Williams, "Coaches Defend Friday Night Hotel Stays," *Lubbock Avalanche-Journal*, Nov. 25, 2009, http://lubbockoneline.com/stories/112509/spo_52860213.shtml.

45   For us, Friday is as big a day as Tuesday.: Williams, "Coaches Defend Friday Night Hotel Stays."

46   and was immediately pressured. . . . replaced by a loud groan.: Don Williams, "Tech Leaves 'Huskers Shell-Shucked," *Lubbock Avalanche-Journal*, Oct. 9, 2005, http://lubbockonline.com/stories/100905/col_100905021.shtml.

46   I was on my back, . . . we won the ball game.: Williams, "Tech Leaves 'Huskers Shell-Shucked."

47   courtesy of senior David Tairu. . . . the guys have for Wally,": Tommy Magelssen, "Tech's Walk-On Shines," *The Daily Toreador*, March 3, 2011, http://www.dailytoreador.com/sports/article_d2688db4-4556-11e09597-00127992bc8b.html.

47   the Oklahoma head coach . . . until at halftime.": Magelssen, "Tech's Walk-On Shines."

47   You know, it's like of like the movie *Rudy*.: Magelssen, "Tech's Walk-On Shines."

48   "the best game of this college football season,": Austin Murphy, "Red-letter Night," *Sports Illustrated*, Nov. 10, 2008, http://sportsillustrated.cnn.com/vault/article/magazine/MAG1148293/index.htm.

48   as senior Tech quarterback Graham . . . the position for you.": Murphy, "Red-Letter Night."

48   The Tech sideline called . . . saying everybody go deep.: Murphy, "Red-Letter Night."

48   After the game, Longhorn . . . Crabtree was double covered.: Murphy, "Red-Letter Night."

48   Twenty-two yards downfield, . . . "dug hard for the end zone,": Murphy, "Red-Letter Night."

48   They tried to man up Crab. [Nobody] can man up Crab.: Murphy, "Red-Letter Night."

49   "fought the living room . . . programs in the country.": Dykes with Boling, *Spike Dykes's Tales*, p. 22.

49   "We knew how . . . be to our program,": Dykes with Boling, *Spike Dykes's Tales*, p. 23.

49   When Hanspard told Rick . . . high fives all around.: Dykes with Boling, *Spike Dykes's Tales*, p. 25.

49   Dad was so sure he . . . wanted to come with us.: Dykes with Boling, *Spike Dykes's Tales*, p. 25.

50   Tech's head football coach . . . to coach without pay.: Sellmeyer and Davidson, p. 138.

50   Assistant coach Walker Nichols left . . . his stint in the Navy.: Sellmeyer and Davidson, p. 142.

50   The Border Conference . . . Tech the league title.: Sellmeyer and Davidson, p. 143.

196

50	Injuries and active duty . . . a 235-lb. former Tech lineman.: Sellmeyer and Davidson, p. 144.
50	When Gillenwater, end . . . by realigning his team.: Sellmeyer and Davidson, p. 145.
50	By the time the season . . . could find on the line.: Sellmeyer and Davidson, p. 154.
50	When practice started for . . . eighty players showed up.: Snellmeyer and Davidson, p. 155.
50	The Navy raided our squad and then the Raiders raided us.: Sellmeyer and Davidson, p. 148.
51	the oldest player on the . . . was all of 3 years old.: Mechelle Voepel, "Lady Raiders Inspired by '93 Champs," *espnW*, Feb. 27, 2013, http://espn.go.com/womens-college-basketball/story/_/id/8991034.
51	"We're just hungry,": Voepel, "Lady Raiders Inspired."
51	"It's important for every team . . . need to play that hard.: Voepel, "Lady Raiders Inspired."
51	I think you embrace the past; you don't run from it or ignore it.: Voepel, "Lady Raiders Inspired."
52	"singularly memorable plays and fantastic finishes.": Don Williams, "Tech's Great Late; Aggies Left in Wake," *Lubbock Avalanche-Journal*, Oct. 5, 2003, http://lubbockonline.com/stories/100503/col_100503017.shtml.
52	"There must be some type . . . just can't explain it.": Patrick Gonzales, "Aggies Unable to Solve Red Raiders in Loss," *Lubbock Avalanche-Journal*, Oct. 6, 2003, http://lubbockonline.com/stories/100603/col_100603016.shtml.
52	It's a weird deal.: Patrick Gonzales, "Aggies Unable to Solve Red Raiders in Loss."
53	DeWitt had observed that . . . you and I can work out.": Sellmeyer and Davidson, p. 208.
53	An expert horseman,: David Murrah, "Tech's First Red Raider," *The Texas Techsan*, Oct.-Nov. 1980, p. 11, http://www.swco.ttu.edu/University_Archive/pdf/1980.pdf.
53	He first borrowed a horse . . . the Levelland Sheriff's Posse: "Texas Tech Masked Rider Program History," *Texas Tech University Center for Campus Life Spirit Program*, http://www.depts.ttu.edu/centerforcampuslife/spiritsquads/MR_hitory.php.
53	he assembled his costume of . . . for the game by train.: Sellmeyer and Davidson, pp. 208-09.
53	was met by stunned disbelief . . . made a more sensational entrance.": "Texas Tech Masked Rider Program History."
53	"the Masked Rider is uniquely Texas Tech.": "Texas Tech Masked Rider Program History."
53	[The Masked Rider] represents one of . . . Tech, but at any university.: "Texas Tech Masked Rider Program History."
54	"I didn't have much experience . . . pitfalls lying in wait,": Leach with Feldman, *Swing Your Sword*, p. 108.
54	"a total distraction for . . . "We ended up playing poorly,": Leach with Feldman, *Swing Your Sword*, p. 109.
54	The idea was, we . . . second interview. Bad idea.: Leach with Feldman, *Swing Your Sword*, p. 109.
55	in February 2007 when she . . . or in my abilities.": Patrick Gonzales, "Cancer Can't Keep Knight from Nationals," *Lubbock Avalanche-Journal*, June 6, 2007, http://lubbockonline.com/stories/060607/col_060607006.shtml.
55	During one competition that . . . went back to work.: "Patience Knight of Texas Tech Wins 2008 Honda Inspiration Award," *Missouri Runner & Triathlete*, May 14, 2008, www.morunandtri.com/read_new/patience-knight.
55	In Patience [Knight], we have the example of someone who won't quit.: "Patience Knight of Texas Tech Wins 2008 Honda Inspiration Award."
56	"That was the first [time] I've ever been around something like that.": Don Williams, "Time to Celebrate," *Lubbock Avalanche-Journal*, Nov. 19, 2007, http://lubbockonline.com/stories/111907/col_111907017.shtml.
56	Thousands of fans, . . . stuff like that.": Williams, "Time to Celebrate."
56	It was great. I didn't want to leave the field.: Williams, "Time to Celebrate."
57	who did not fumble a single time the season before: Doug Hensley, "Unlikely Fumble Dissolved Upset-Minded Bulldogs' Hopes," *Lubbock Avalanche-Journal*, Sept. 20, 1998, http://lubbockonline.com/stories/092098/064-2345.shtml.
57	Sometimes it's better to be lucky than good.: Sam Scott, "Tech, Shipley Recover for 3-0 Start," *Lubbock Avalanche-Journal*, Sept. 20, 1998, http://lubbockonline.com/stories/092098/0920980038.shtml.
58	As June 2008 began, . . . thinking about Tech baseball.: George Watson, "Larry Hays Ends 22-Year Love Affair with Texas Tech Baseball," *Lubbock Avalanche-Journal*, June 3, 2008, http://lubbockonline.com/stories/060308/spo_285725492.shtml.
58	"For years, and this may . . . we felt abused.": Jared Parcell, "A Legendary Red Raider: Tech's Diamond-Men Shined," in *Raiding the SWC*, p. 143.
58	"When we go places . . . top teams in the country.": Parcell in *Raiding the SWC*, p. 143.
58	Something about staying . . . handed in his resignation.: Watson, "Larry Hays

	Ends 22-Year Love Affair."
58	I always asked (friends) how will I know, what is the sign? (One) way is you just know.: Watson, "Larry Hays Ends 22-Year Love Affair."
59	Before the 1926 season . . . were presented with blankets: Sellmeyer and Davidson, p. 28.
59	The season featured the first . . . for the TCU game.: Sellmeyer and Davidson, pp. 29-30.
59	The contest against Schreiner . . . had never been blown dead.: Sellmeyer and Davidson, p. 29.
60	After each injury, a disappointed . . . he was their guy.: Chris Mahr, "A Chance Worth Waiting For," *Sports Illustrated*, Aug. 26, 2012, http://sportsillustrated.cnn.com/vault/article/magazine/MAG1203473/index.htm.
60	We knew that it was going to take some time.: Mahr, "A Chance Worth Waiting For."
61	The school's athletic facilities . . . Border Conference standards.": Sellmeyer and Davidson, p. 268.
61	King always insisted that . . . over Texas in 1967.: Sellmeyer and Davidson, p. 269.
61	So many fans met the . . . the crowd to disperse.: Sellmeyer and Davidson, p. 311.
61	"We do not choose whether . . . on which we will stand.": R. Alan Culpepper, "The Gospel of Luke: Introduction, Commentary, and Reflections," *The New Interpreter's Bible*, Vol. IX (Nashville: Abingdon Press, 1998), p. 153.
61	He is the man who . . . foundation for Texas Tech.: Sellmeyer and Davidson, p. 272.
62	With 45 seconds left on . . . a 3 from the right wing.: Randy Rosetta, "Raiders Stun No. 22 Sooners," *Lubbock Avalanche-Journal*, Jan. 17, 2001, http://lubbockonline.com/stories/011701/spo_011701063.shtml.
62	"I thought about whether . . . early in the shot clock.": Jeremy Cowen, "Brown Takes Full Advantage of Second Chance," *Lubbock Avalanche-Journal*, Jan. 17, 2001, http://lubbockonline.com/stories/011701/spo_011701064.shtml.
62	calling for two different . . . the defense OU employed.: Rosetta, "Raiders Stun No. 22."
62	Brown calmly brought . . . ticked down to 8 seconds.: Cowen, "Brown Takes Full Advantage."
62	when no one moved over . . . spinning 5-foot bank shot: Rosetta, "Raiders Stun No. 22."
62	He couldn't see it, . . . with a massive roar.: Cowen, "Brown Takes Full Advantage."
62	I looked up at the . . . going to need a prayer.: Cowen, "Brown Takes Full Advantage."
63	"The word is the one . . . throws the ball very good,": Brent Schrotenboer, "Welker Hornswoggles UT," *Lubbock Avalanche-Journal*, Nov. 17, 2002, http://lubbockonline.com/stories/111702/col_1117020018.shtml.
63	when Welker leaned over . . . they blitzed a safety.: Schrotenboer, "Welker Hornswoggles UT."
63	Welker made the suggestion. . . . get the ball a lot.: Schrotenboer, "Welker Hornswoggles UT."
64	the A&M offense "sliced and diced": Don Williams, "Raiders Control Second Half vs. Aggies," *Lubbock Avalanche-Journal*, Oct 19, 2008, http://lubbockonline.com/stories/10908/spo_346105147.shtml.
64	"typically raucous and swaying": Williams, "Raiders Control Second Half."
64	"It was more of a . . . and that's what happened.: Williams, "Raiders Control Second Half."
64	I was proud of them for that.: Williams, "Raiders Control Second Half."
65	Tech's admission to the . . . to split his team up.: Sellmeyer and Davidson, p. 69.
65	Under the conference's eligibility . . . to play against New Mexico Normal.: Sellmeyer and Davidson, p. 70.
65	Seeking a large crowd for . . . admitted free of charge.: Sellmeyer and Davidson, p. 70.
65	As soon as the game ended, Cawthon boarded a train: Sellmeyer and Davidson, p. 70.
66	Thomas played that day despite . . . mother showed up to nurse him.: Dykes with Boling, *Spike Dykes's Tales*, p. 116.
66	a "slow-footed, undersized" player destined for some junior college.: Scott Howard- Cooper, "Not Mapped Out," *Los Angles Times*, Dec. 27, 1994, http://articles/latimes/com/1994-12-27/sports/sp-13391_1_texas-tech.
66	The Tech coaches were . . . kind of kid we want.": Dykes with Boling, *Spike Dykes's Tales*, p. 31.
66	Zach Thomas wasn't recruited . . . with a player like Zach Thomas.: Dykes with Boling, *Spike Dykes's Tales*, p. 22.
67	The ball bounced away . . . ESPN2 carried the game.: Courtney Linehan, "Case of the Stolen Ball," *Lubbock Avalanche-Journal*, Dec. 6, 2009, http://lubbockonline.com/stories/120609/spo_53271805.shtml.
67	The Raiders were in the . . . return to the court.: Linehan, "Case of the Stolen Ball."
67	The fans and the debris they left behind had to be cleared: "Texas Tech Knocks off No. 10 Washington," *ESPN.com*, Dec. 3, 2009, http://espn.go.com/ncb/ecap?gameid=293372641.
67	The student managers managed to . . . for use in the game.: Linehan, "Case of the Stolen Ball."
67	I really thought my life . . . I was dead meat.: Linehan, "Case of the Stolen Ball."
69	the thought of transferring . . . be the starter after [2000],": Don Williams, "Symons Demonstrates Example of Patience Paying Dividends," *Lubbock Avalanche-Journal*, Nov. 1, 2003, http://

	lubbockonline.com/stories/110103/col_110103007.shtml.
69	"a poster boy for delayed gratification.": Williams, "Symons Demonstrates Example of Patience."
69	His patience and his . . . he is right now.: Williams, "Symons Demonstrates Example of Patience."
70	"I'm more excited about . . . a personal foul penalty.: "Tech Football Notes: McNeal in Check," *Lubbock Avalanche-Journal*, Nov. 6, 2005, http://lubbockonline.com/stories/110605/col_110605026.shtml.
70	We were right where we wanted to be at halftime.: Patrick Gonzales, "Things Go Sour for Aggies in Second Half," *Lubbock Avalanche-Journal*, Nov. 6, 2005, http://lubbockonline.com/stories/110605/col_110605027.shtml.
71	Texas Tech cross-country coach . . . for his program "revolutionary.": Kate Meriwether, "Texas Tech Student-Athlete Spotlight: Sally Kipyego," *Big12Sports.com*, Nov. 18, 2008, http://www.big12sports.com/ViewArticle.dbml?ATCLID=1627253.
71	As a young girl, she . . . better health care there.": Tim Griffin, "Inspired by Early Tragedy, Kipyego Is Running for a Cause," *ESPN.com*, June 10, 2008, http://sports.espn.go.com/ncaa/story?id=3434411.
71	Some days her rounds . . . to take care of.: Meriwether, "Texas Tech Student-Athlete Spotlight."
71	She [took] both the . . . we've never been.: Meriwether, "Texas Tech Student-Athlete Spotlight"
72	personally interviewing 49 . . . to about 150 coaches.: Sellmeyer and Davidson, p. 331.
72	he said he was one of the . . . a close look at his spiritual life.": "Jim Carlen," *Wikipedia, the free encyclopedia*, http://en.wikipedia.org/wiki/Jim_Carlen.
72	"My coaches and I discuss . . . but I do request it,": Sellmeyer and Davidson, p. 330.
72	The student underground . . . weight, not his faith.: Sellmeyer and Davidson, p. 333.
72	When you have God on your side, you don't have to worry.: "Jim Carlen," *Wikipedia*.
73	the greatest comeback in the Tech history.: Don Williams, "Raiders Strike Late Again," *Lubbock Avalanche-Journal*, Sept. 26, 2004, http://lubbockonline.com/stories/092604/col_092604016.shtml.
73	tying the record for biggest comeback: Williams, "Raiders Strike Late Again."
73	"He kind of took us all by surprise, making that call,": Williams, "Raiders Strike Late Again."
73	"I saw daylight, and I hit it,": Williams, "Raiders Strike Late Again."
73	I had to check with [Mike Leach] to make sure that's what he wanted.: Williams, "Raiders Strike Late Again."
74	the groan of the Jones Stadium crowd was audible.: Randy Rosetta, "McCann Energizes Tech in Win," *Lubbock Avalanche-Journal*, Sept. 9, 2001, http://lubbockonline.com/stories/090901/col_0909010009.shtml.
74	Tech special teams coach . . . the sideline, "No, no, no!": Jeremy Cowen, "McCann's Run Helps Pump Tech Up," *Lubbock Avalanche-Journal*, Sept. 9, 2001, http://lubbockonline.com/stories/090901/col_0909010011.shtml.
74	"Against the wishes of . . . "Go, go, go!" Cowen, "McCan's Run Helps Pump Tech Up."
74	eluded a gang of Lobos . . . New Mexico kicker at the 45: Rosetta, "McCann Energizes Tech."
74	"That play turned the entire game around,": Rosetta, "McCann Energizes Tech."
74	I don't know if . . . as I was the run.: Cowen, "McCann's Run Helps Pump Tech Up."
75	"He's not your average cat,": Brandon Chatmon, "DeAndre Washington Brings a Constant to Texas Tech's Offense," *ESPN.com*, July 22, 2015, http://espn.go.com/blog/big12/post/_/id/101289/deandre-washington-brings-a-constant-to-texas-techs-offense.
75	"I just want to say . . . to go score again.": Don Williams, "Washington Learned His Lesson," *Red Raiders.com*, Sept. 17, 2013, http://redraiders.com/sports-red-raiders-football/2013-09-17/williams-washington-learned-his-lesson.
75	Not a big deal. Go make a play.: Williams, "Washington Learned His Lesson."
76	"I thought I was always . . . stuff I had to grasp,": Don Williams, "Former Red Raider Took Advantage of Rare Switch," *Avalanche-Journal*, Oct. 9, 2005, http://lubbockonline.com/stories/100905/col_100905022.shtml.
76	"He broke, three, four, . . . to count 'em up.": Williams, "Former Red Raider Took Advantage of Rare Switch."
76	You don't see a lot . . . tight end to running back.: Williams, "Former Red Raider Took Advantage of Rare Switch."
77	He once removed all the . . . Take a choice.": Sellmeyer and Davidson, p. 50.
77	He posted a set of rules . . . Watch your digestion very closely.: Sellmeyer and Davidson, p. 52.
77	6) Get out early when . . . workout and little at that.: Sellmeyer and Davidson, p. 53.
77	These rules and regulations are . . . jelly and a wisher.: Sellmeyer and Davidson, p. 53.
78	With less than 90 seconds . . a perfect 4-for-4.: Jose Rodriguez, "Doege Sets Record," *The Daily Toreador*, Sept. 18, 2011. http://www.dailytoreador.com/sports/article_03918df4-e26a-11e0-9981-0019bb30f31a.html.

78	On Tech's second possession, . . . what we're here to do.": Rodriguez, "Doege Sets Record."
78	to run his completion streak . . . on a fade route.: Rodriguez, "Doege Sets Record."
78	he completed a screen . . . in for that last pass.: Rodriguez, "Doege Sets Record."
79	Asked by his mom . . . one word to say: "Blessed.": Greg Bishop, "How Matt Mooney Became the Perfect Piece to Texas Tech's Final Four Puzzle," *SI.com*, April 4,2019, https://www.si.com/college/2019/04/04/texas-tech-red-raiders-matt-mooney-chris-beard.
79	"was a main factor in Tech's unprecedented season.": Bishop, "How Matt Mooney Became."
79	the summer before he . . . to the NCAA Tournament.": Bishop, "How Matt Mooney Became."
79	Classic Matthew.: Bishop, "How Matt Mooney Became."
80	Mike Leach told his team . . . a chance to make history. "Down 31, Texas Tech Rallies," *ESPN*, Dec. 29, 2006, http://sports.espn.go.com/ncf/recap?gameId=263630135.
80	I knew it was kind . . . behind to win this thing.: "Down 31, Texas Tech Rallies."
81	"a sea of goat grass, thistles, . . . the toughest football player.": Sellmeyer and Davidson, p. 14.
81	A vacant lot just off the . . . a more permanent site.: Sellmeyer and Davidson, p. 15.
81	A garage apartment at the end of . . . would trot along behind.": Sellmeyer and Davidson, pp. 15-16.
81	"there were fewer grass burrs . . . than on the Tech campus.: Sellmeyer and Davidson, p. 17.
81	At halftime, the teams gathered . . . either end of the playing field.: Sellmeyer and Davidson, p. 21.
81	The conditions under which . . . would seem almost barbaric: Sellmeyer and Davidson, p. 14.
82	he existed "on the . . . before you get pablum.": Dykes with Boling, *Spike Dykes's Tales*, p. 107.
82	The coach's heart surgeon told him that he needed surgery — immediately.: Dykes with Boling, *Spike Dykes's Tales*, p. 108.
82	He had six bypasses . . . our workout and films,": Dykes with Boling, *Spike Dykes's Tales*, p. 109.
82	"a group of electrical . . . with those people, too.": Dykes with Boling, *Spike Dykes's Tales*, p. 110.
82	If you say you're . . . you need to do it.: Dykes with Boling, *Spike Dykes's Tales*, p. 110.
83	Richards declared his commitment . . . or were big Tech fans.": Don Williams, "Playing for Red Raiders all that Richards Ever Wanted," *Lubbock Avalanche-Journal*, Oct. 27, 2014, http://lubbockonline.com/sports-red-raiders-football/2014-10-17/playing-red-raides-all-richards-ever-wanted#.VeBq-PlViko.
83	It's just the culture I grew up in.: Williams, "Playing for Red Raiders."
84	Thurman followed blocks by . . . down the sideline: "Texas Tech Surprises Texas A&M," *The Washington Post*, Oct. 4, 1987, http://www.highbeam.com/doc/1P2-1346733.html.
84	Myers offered Thurman a . . . nationally ranked Razorbacks.: Kirk Baird, "A Legendary Red Raider: Tech Found a Football Giant," in *Raiding the SWC*, p. 64.
84	Thurman always declared . . . for the first down.: Baird, "A Legendary Red Raider: Tech Found a Football Giant," p. 64.
84	When people question my . . . It pushes me harder.: Baird, "A Legendary Red Raider: Tech Found a Football Giant," p. 64.
85	"We didn't always have the best team, but we always had the best announcer.": Don Williams, "A Legend Lost," *Lubbock Avalanche-Journal*, July 29, 2011, http://lubbockonline.com/sports-red-raiders/2011-07-29.
85	He recalled that often . . . Kansas City radio trade school.: Don Williams, "A Legend Lost."
85	He sent letters to 113 . . . had ever listened to.: Don Williams, "A Legend Lost.
85	It was ordained for me to come to KFYO in Lubbock.: Don Williams, "A Legend Lost."
86	Leach said that one attitude . . . sick self-fulfilling prophecy,": Leach with Feldman, *Swing Your Sword*, p. 122.
86	"the Red Raiders just . . . too good to play them.": Leach with Feldman, *Swing Your Sword*, p. 122.
86	In the locker room, the . . . get out of here.": Leach with Feldman, *Swing Your Sword*, pp. 122-23.
86	"He made a big . . . can't take anybody lightly,": Leach with Feldman, *Swing Your Sword*, p. 123.
86	You have to have respect . . . made in the program.: Leach with Feldman, *Swing Your Sword*, p. 123.
87	few big-time programs . . . except for Tech.: Don Williams, "Francis Finds New Challenge on Golf Course," *Lubbock Avalanche-Journal*, Oct. 19, 2002, http://lubbockonline.com/stories/101902/col_1019020036.shtml.
87	Francis patterned himself . . . what Rice would do.: Williams, "Francis Finds New Challenge on Golf Course."
87	he decided to take up . . . I still haven't shot 79.": Williams, "Francis Finds New Challenge."
87	If you need to give . . . someone you point to.: Williams, "Francis Finds New Challenge."
88	following his junior year, . . . "I recruited him to play linebacker.": Sellmeyer and David-son, p. 299.
88	King called for a sideline . . . the last 37 yards untouched: Sellmeyer and Davidson, p. 295.
88	he broke into tears: Sellmeyer and Davidson, p. 295.
88	I knew one thing; after I caught the ball.: Sellmeyer and Davidson, p. 295.
89	OU was an overwhelming 29-point favorite.: Jimmy Burch, "Texas Tech's Win over OU Is One for

200

the History Books," *Star-Telegram.com*, Oct. 24, 2011, http://nl.newsbank.com/nl-search/we/Archives?p_action=doc&p_docid=13DF7E85653D1.

89   "They whipped us in every part of the game,": Burch, "Texas Tech's Win over OU."

89   "A lot of people thought we couldn't do this,": Burch, "Texas Tech's Win over OU."

89   When you go on the roa dnd beat the No. 1 team, it is really special, . . . almost impossible to do.: Burch, "Texas Tech's Win over OU."

90   They used five different players . . . wanted to take control.": Milton Kent, "Swoopes' Record 47 Points Power Texas Tech to Title," *The Baltimore Sun*, April 5, 1993, articles.baltimoresun.com/1993-04-05/sports/1993095104_1_sheryl-swoopes-texas-tech-championship-game.

90   With 58 seconds left, . . . let her go to work.: Kent, "Swoopes' Record 47 Points Power Texas Tech."

90   "It's the greatest feeling any of us have had in our athletic careers,": Kent, "Swoopes' Record 47 Points Power Texas Tech."

90   There are no words . . . a player Sheryl Swoopes is.: Kent, "Swoopes' Record 47 Points Power Texas Tech."

91   "green as a gourd" . . . all different subjects.: Dykes with Boling, *Spike Dykes's Tales*, p. 39.

91   He was fired "almost . . . tossed their sandwich bags around.": Dykes with Boling, *Spike Dykes's Tales*, p. 40.

91   he announced that the next guy . . . he finish out the school year.: Dykes with Boling, *Spike Dykes's Tales*, p. 41.

91   "There's a lot worse things . . . were part of the coaching profession.: Dykes with Boling, *Spike Dykes's Tales*, p. 41.

91   I was never afraid about . . . about what was going to happen.: Dykes with Boling, *Spike Dykes's Tales*, p. 41.

92   Our offense did a . . . of snowballing for us.": Don Williams, "No. 20. Texas Tech Beats Kansas," *Lubbock Avalanche-Journal*, Oct. 5, 2013. http://lubbockonline.com/filed-online/2013-10-05/no-20-texas-tech-beats-kansas-54-16#.Vd8dXvlViko.

92   Getting started is the . . . we're on a roll.: Williams, "No. 20 Texas Tech Beats Kansas."

93   "acted as crazed as ranch . . . West Texas heat too long.": Ron Reid, "A Real Lulu in Lubbock," *Sports Illustrated*, Nov. 8, 1976, http://sportsillustrated.cnn.com/vault/article/magazine/MAG1091756/index.htm.

93   even to the tune of paying . . . to the rubber room.": Reid, "A Real Lulu in Lubbock."

93   "I don't feel I'm a first-class passer.": Reid, "A Real Lulu in Lubbock."

93   "As long as there is . . . hurt his toes one bit.: Reid, "A Real Lulu in Lubbock."

93   "We've got something here that's exciting,": Reid, "A Real Lulu in Lubbock."

93   Lubbock's lunacy hit a new bonkers level.: Reid, "A Real Lulu in Lubbock."

94   "I wasn't happy,": "Cumbie Throws for 441 Yards to Rout Frogs," *ESPN.com*, Sept. 25, 2004, http://scores.espn.go.com/ncf/recap?gameId=242622641.

94   Leach "gave us some profound words.": Don Williams, "Texas Tech Football Notebook: Players Who Turned Coach," *Lubbock Avalanche-Journal*, Oct. 23, 2014. http://lubbockonline.com/sports/2014-10-23/texas-tech-football-notebook-players-who-turned-coach-recall-04-tech-tcu-scene#.VeBx0PlViko.

94   "Leach called us [over] . . . about a hundred times,": Williams, "Texas Tech Football Notebook."

94   "We knew it would snowball once it started,": "Cumbie Throws for 441 Yards to Rout Frogs."

94   We had a little run . . . and won the game.: Williams, "Texas Tech Football Notebook."

95   For some time, the Tech athletic . . . more than a handful of Texas teams.: Sellmeyer and Davidson, p. 129.

95   The proposed 1941 schedule also . . . state programs wouldn't play Tech: Sellmeyer and Davidson, p. 129.

95   Cawthon and his players came home . . . a game with undefeated Hardin-Simmons.: Sellmeyer and Davidson, p. 128.

95   Cawthon and assistant Dutchey Smith . . . the idea of playing Hardin-Simmons.: Sellmeyer and Davidson, p. 129.

95   When Cawthon submitted his . . . era in Texas Tech football.: Sellmeyer and Davidson, p. 129.

WORKS CITED

Anderson, Kelli. "Tech Knockout." *Sports Illustrated*. 28 March 2005. http://sportsillustrated.cnn.com/vault/article/magazine/MAG1110341/index.htm.

Baird, Kirk. "A Legendary Red Raider: Tech Found a Football Giant in All-American Punt Returner Tyrone 'Smurf' Thurman." in *Raiding the SWC: The Collective History of Red Raider Sports in the Southwest Conference*. Gina Augustini, Kent Best, Darrel Thomas, eds. Lubbock: Texas Tech Student Publications, 1996. 64.

Beilue, Jon Mark. "'The Best College Football Player in America.'" *Amarillo Globe-News*. 26 Dec. 1999. http://amarillo.com/stories/122699/spo_170-7178.shtml.

Bishop, Greg. "How Matt Mooney Became the Perfect Piece to Texas Tech's Final Four Puzzle." *SI.com*. 4 April 2019. https://www.si.com/college/2019/04/04/texas-tech-red-raiders-matt-mooney-chris-beard.

Burch, Jimmy. "Texas Tech's Win over OU Is One for the History Books." *Star-Telegram.com*. 24 Oct. 2011. http://nl.newsbank.com/nl-search/we/Archives?p_action=doc&p_docid=13DF7E85653D1.

Carriger, Linda. "A Legendary Red Raider: Sheryl Swoopes Propelled Lady Raiders to the Greatest Feat of All — a National Title." in *Raiding the SWC: The Collective History of Red Raider Sports in the Southwest Conference*. Gina Augustini, Kent Best, Darrel Thomas, eds. Lubbock: Texas Tech Student Publications, 1996. 124.

Cash, Rana L. "Texas Tech Investigates Wes Welker Tweets to Recruit Nick Kurtz." *Sporting News*. 12 June 2013. http://www.sportingnews.com/ncaa-football/story/2013-06-12.

Chatmon, Brandon. "DeAndre Washington Brings a Constant to Texas Tech's Offense." *ESPN.com*. 22 July 2015. http://espn.go.com/blog/big12/post/_/id/101289/deandre-washington-brings-a-constant-to-texas-techs-offense.

"Chris Williams Profile." *TexasTech.com*. http://www.texastech.com/sports/m-basebl/mtt/williams_chris 00.html.

"Cody Fuller." *ZoomInfo.com*. http://www.zoominfo.com/p/Cody-Fuller/86115961.

Cowen, Jeremy. "Brown Takes Full Advantage of Second Chance." *Lubbock Avalanche-Journal*. 17 Jan. 2001. http://lubbockonline.com/stories/011701/spo_011701063.shtml.

-----. "McCann's Run Helps Pump Tech Up." *Lubbock Avalanche-Journal*. 9 Sept. 2001. http://lubbockonline.com/stories/090901/col_0909010011.shtml.

Culpepper, R. Alan. "The Gospel of Luke: Introduction, Commentary, and Reflections." *The New Interpreter's Bible*. Vol. IX. Nashville: Abingdon Press, 1998. 1-490.

"Cumbie Throws for 441 Yards to Rout Frogs." *ESPN.com*. 25 Sept. 2014. http://scores.espn.go.com/ncf/recap?gameId=242622641.

"Down 31, Texas Tech Rallies for Biggest Bowl Comeback." *ESPN*. 29 Dec. 2006. http://sports.espn.go/com/ncf/recap?gameId=263630135.

DuPont, Michael II. "Kingsbury Welcomed as New Head Football Coach In United Spirit Arena." *The Daily Toreador*. 14 Dec. 2012, http://www.dailytoreador.com/news/article_1bd6becc-4626-11e2-8d4a-0019bb30f31a.html.

-----. "Red Raiders Dominate Mountaineers, 49-14, in Homecoming Game." *The Daily Toreador*. 15 Oct. 2012. http://www.dailytoreador.com/sports/article-26bded1c-15b4-11e2-a3f7-001a4bcf6878.html.

Dykes, Spike with Dave Boling. *Spike Dykes's Tales from the Texas Tech Sideline*. Champaign, Ill.: Sports Publishing L.L.C., 2004.

Elsen, Emily. "A Legendary Red Raider: Darvin Ham Served Up a Shattering Ham Slam That Dunked North Carolina." in *Raiding the SWC: The Collective History of Red Raider Sports in the Southwest Conference*. Gina Augustini, Kent Best, Darrel Thomas, eds. Lubbock: Texas Tech Student Publications, 1996. 106.

Gonzales, Patrick. "Aggies Unable to Solve Red Raiders in Loss." *Lubbock Avalanche-Journal*. 6 Oct. 2003. http://lubbockonline.com/stories/100603/col_100603016.shtml.

-----. "Cancer Can't Keep Knight from Nationals." *Lubbock Avalanche-Journal*. 6 June 2007. http://lubbockonline.com/stories/060607/col_060607006.shtml.

-----. "Looking Back: Lady Raiders Win National Championship." *Texas Tech Today*. 17 Feb. 2013. http://today.ttu.edu/2013/02/looking-back.

-----. "Runner Finds Inspiration Under Tutelage of Tech Coach." *Lubbock Avalanche-Journal*. 25 May 2007. http://lubbockonline.com/stories/052507/col_052507084.shtml.

-----. "Things Go Sour for Aggies in Second Half." *Lubbock Avalanche-Journal*. 6 Nov. 2005. http://lubbockonline.com/stories/110605/col_110605027.shtml.

Greenberg, Terry. "Harrell Quiets Raucous Kyle Field Following Leach's 'Pep Talk.'" in "Don Williams' 10 Memorable Moments of the Texas Tech-A&M Rivalry." *RedRaiders.com*. 7 Oct. 2011. http://red

raiders.com/sports-red-raiders-football/2011-10-07.

Griffin, Steven. "Miscues, Turnovers Almost Ruin Big Day." *Lubbock Avalanche-Journal*. 28 Sept. 2003. http://lubbockonline.com/stories/092803/col_092803011.shtml.

Griffin, Tim. "Inspired by Early Tragedy, Kipyego Is Running for a Cause." *ESPN.com*. 10 June 2008. http://sports.espn.go.com/ncaa/news/story?id=3434411.

Hengst, Max. "Brooks Steps up as Leader, Star Player for Tech's Defense." *thedailytoreador.com*. 9 Oct. 2019. http://www.dailytoreador.com/sports.brooks-steps-up-as-leader-star-player-for-tech.

Hensley, Doug. "Unlikely Fumble Dissolved Upset-Minded Bulldogs' Hopes." *Lubbock Avalanche-Journal*. 20 Sept. 1998. http://lubbockonline.com/stories/092098/064-2345.shtml.

Howard-Cooper, Scott. "Not Mapped Out: Thomas Brothers Take Bizarre Route to Cotton Bowl-Bound Texas Tech." *Los Angeles Times*. 27 Dec. 1994. http://articles.latimes.com/1994-12-27/sports/sp-3391_1_texas-tech.

"Jim Carlen." *Wikipedia, the free encyclopedia*. http://en.wikipedia.org/wiki/Jim_Carlen.

Kent, Milton. "Swoopes' Record 47 Points Power Texas Tech to Title." *The Baltimore Sun*. 5 April 1993. articles.baltimoresun.com/1993-04-05/sports/1993095104_1_sheryl-swoopes-texas-tech-championship-game.

Leach, Mike with Bruce Feldman. *Swing Your Sword: Leading the Charge in Football and Life*. New York City: Diversion Books, 2012.

Leeson, JT. "A Texas Tech Legend." *TexasTech.com*. 12 Oct. 2001. http://www.texastech.com/sports/m-footbl/spec-rel/101201aaa.html.

Lewis, Michael. "Coach Leach Goes Deep, Very Deep." *The New York Times*. 4 Dec. 2005. http://www.nytimes.com/2005/12/04/magazine/04coach.html.

"Lighthearted Linemen Contrast Leach's Harsh Remarks." *Lubbock Avalanche-Journal*. 16 Sept. 2008. http://lubbockonline.com/stories/091608/spo_332866621.shtml.

Linehan, Courtney. "Case of the Stolen Ball: Tech Scrambles as Game Ball Is Grabbed." *Lubbock Avalanche-Journal*. 6 Dec. 2009. http://lubbockonline.com/stories/120609/spo_53271805.shtml.

-----. "Start to Finish, Raiders Run Over Sooners." *Lubbock Avalanche-Journal*. 22 Nov. 2009. http://lubbockonline.com/112209/spo_527630721.shtml.

"Louisville Becomes Latest No. 1 to Lose, Falls to Texas Tech." *SI.com*. 11 Dec. 2019. https://www.si.com/college/college-basketball/game/2164434.

MacArthur, John. *Twelve Ordinary Men*. Nashville: W Publishing Group, 2002.

Magelssen, Tommy. "1993 Team Came Mostly from West Texas, But It Was Lubbock and Marsha Sharp That Reeled Them In." *Lubbock Avalanche-Journal*. 16 Feb. 2013. http://lubbockonline.com/sports-red-raiders-womens-basketball/2013-02-15.

-----. "Tech Upends UH 35-20 to End Regular Season." *The Daily Toreador*. 28 Nov. 2010. http://www.thedailytoreador.com/sports/article_f099558a-fb5e-11df-8cd1-00127992bc8b.html.

-----. "Tech's Walk-On Shines During Senior Night." *The Daily Toreador*. 3 March 2011. http://www.dailytoreador.com/sports/article_d2688db4-4556-11e0-9597-00127992bc8b.html.

Mahr, Chris. "A Chance Worth Waiting For." *Sports Illustrated*. 16 Aug. 2012. http://sportsillustrated.cnn.com/vault/article/magazine/MAG1203473/index.htm.

-----. "Putting His Career in Flight." *Sports Illustrated*. 12 Aug. 2011. http://sportsillustrated.cnn.com/vault/article/magazine/MAG1188661/index.htm.

Maisel, Ivan. "The Good Life of Kliff Kingsbury." *ESPN.com*. 4 July 2013. http://espn.go.com/college-football/story/_/id9447111.

Meriwether, Kate. "Texas Tech Student-Athlete Spotlight: Sally Kipyego." *Big12Sports.com*. 18 Nov. 2008. http://www.big12sports.com/ViewArticle.dbml?ATCLID=1627253.

Murphy, Austin. "Red-letter Night." *Sports Illustrated*. 10 Nov. 2008. http://sportsillustrated.cnn.com/vault/article/magazine/MAG 1148293/index.htm.

Murrah, David. "Tech's First Red Raider." *The Texas Techsan*. Oct.-Nov. 1980. 11. http://www.swco.ttu.edu/University_Archive/pdf/1980.pdf.

Parcell, Jared." "A Legendary Red Raider: Tech's Diamond-Men Shined Brightly in SWC Under Coach Larry Hays." in *Raiding the SWC: The Collective History of Red Raider Sports in the Southwest Conference*. Gina Augustini, Kent Best, Darrel Thomas, eds. Lubbock: Texas Tech Student Publications, 1996. 143.

"Patience Knight of Texas Tech Wins 2008 Honda Inspiration Award." *Missouri Runner & Triathlete*. 14 May 2008. www.morunandtri.com/read_new/patience-knight.

Posner, Jay. "Captain Gave Raiders Berth in Sweet Sixteen." *The San Diego Union-Tribune*. 22 March 2005. htttp://www.utsandiego.com/uniontrib/20050322/news_1s22ncaa.html.

"Raiders Get Their Turn to Celebrate." *Lubbock Avalanche-Journal*. 22 Nov. 2009. http://lubbockonline.com/stories/11209/spo_527631907.shtml.

Reid, Ron. "A Real Lulu in Lubbock." *Sports Illustrated*. 8 Nov. 1976. http://sports

203

illustrated.cnn.com/vault/article/magazine/MAG1091756/index.htm.

Rodriguez, Jose. "Doege Sets Record, Goes 40-for-44 Passing at UNM." *The Daily Toreador.* 18 Sept. 2011. http://www.dailytoreador.com/sports/article_03918df4-e26a-11e0-9981-0019bb30f31a.html.

-----. "Red Raiders Upset No. 14 Missouri Tigers." *The Daily Toreador.* 7 Nov. 2010. http://www.daily toreador.com/sports/article_fcb72900-ead3-11df-9229-00127992bc8b.html.

-----. "Tech D Proves Worth, Pressures QB Smith Throughout Win." *The Daily Toreador.* 15 Oct. 2012. http://www.dailytoreador.com/sports/article-0d04b184-168c-11e2-9d17-001a4bcf6878.html.

Rosetta. Randy. "Knight 'Livid' over Tech Situation." *Lubbock Avalanche-Journal.* 11 March 2001. http://lubbockonline.com/stories/031101/spo_031101114.shtml.

-----. "McCann Energizes Tech in Win." *Lubbock Avalanche-Journal.* 9 Sept. 2001. http: //lubbockonline.com/stories/090901/col_0909010009.shtml.

-----. "Raiders Stun No. 22 Sooners." *Lubbock Avalanche-Journal.* 17 Jan. 2001. http://lubbockonline.com/stories/011701/spo_011701063.shtml.

-----. "Tech Players Get Taste of Knight Life." *Lubbock Avalanche-Journal.* 25 March 2001. http://lubbock online.com/stories/032501/col_032501022.shtml.

-----. "Williams, Tech Bury Bears." *Lubbock Avalanche-Journal.* 28 Oct. 2001. http://lubbockonline.com/stories/102801/col_1028010013.shtml.

Schrotenboer, Brent. "Raiders' Magic Comes Back to Haunt Aggies." *Lubbock Avalanche-Journal.* 6 Oct. 2002. http://lubbockonline.com/stories/100602/col_1006020016.shtml.

-----. "Welker Hornswoggles UT." *Lubbock Avalanche-Journal.* 17 Nov. 2002. http://lubbockonline.com/stories/111702/col_1117020018.shtml.

Scott, Sam. "Hardaway Relates Tech Experience." *Lubbock Avalanche-Journal.* 7 Feb. 1999. http://lubbock online.com/stories/020799/0207990053.shtml.

-----. "Tech, Shipley Recover for 3-0 Start." *Lubbock Avalanche-Journal.* 20 Sept. 1998. http://lubbockonline.com/stories/092098/0920980038.shtml.

Sellmeyer, Ralph L. and James E. Davidson. *The Red Raiders: Texas Tech Football.* Huntsville, Ala.: The Strode Publishers, Inc., 1978.

Sherman, Rodger. "How Chris Beard Built Texas Tech into College Basketball's Most Unlikely Juggernaut." *TheRinger.com.* 3 April 2019. https://www.theringer.com/march-madness/2019/4/3/18293467/chris-beard-texas-tech-jarrett-culver-final-four-defense.

Suniga, Michael. "Morris Saddened to Leave, Has Unfinished Business on the Court." *The Daily Toreador.* 7 March 2013. http://www.dailytoreador.com/sports/article_aa00f750-87a6-11e2-a02d-001a4b-cf6878.html.

"Tech Football Notes: McNeal in Check." *Lubbock Avalanche-Journal.* 6 Nov. 2005. http://lubbockonline.com/stories/110605/col_110605026.shtml.

"Texas Tech Knocks off No. 10 Washington in OT to Remain Unbeaten." *ESPN.com.* 3 Dec. 2009. http://espn.go.com/ncb/recap?gameid=293372641.

"Texas Tech Masked Rider Program History." *Texas Tech University Center for Campus Life Spirit Program.* http://www.depts.ttu.edu/centerforcampuslife/spiritsquads/MRhistory.php.

"Texas Tech Surprises Texas A&M." *The Washington Post.* 4 Oct. 1987. http://www.highbeam.com/doc/1P2-1346733.html.

Voepel, Mechelle. "Lady Raiders Inspired by '93 Champs." *espnW.* 27 Feb. 2013. http://espn.go.com/womens-college-basketball/story/_/id/8991034.

Watson, George. "Fuller Trades Pads for Glove as Tech Baseball Starts Drills." *Lubbock Avalanche-Journal.* 14 Jan. 2004. http://lubbockonline.com/stories/011404/col_011404017.shtml.

-----. "Larry Hays Ends 22-Year Love Affair with Texas Tech Baseball." *Lubbock Avalanche-Journal.* 3 June 2008. http://lubbockonline.com/stories/060308/spo_285725492.shtml.

"Wes Welker." *Wikipedia, the free encyclopedia.* http://en.wikipedia.org/wiki/Wes_Welker.

Westbrook, Ray. "E.J. Holub Is Famous Both for Football and For His Horse." *Lubbock Avalanche-Journal.* 10 Feb. 2013. http://lubbockonline.com/life-columnists/2013-02-10.

Williams, Don. "A Legend Lost: Jack Dale, a Texas Tech Fixture on Lubbock Airwaves Since 1952, Died Friday Evening." *Lubbock Avalanche-Journal.* 29 July 2011. http://lubbockonline.com/sports-red-raiders/2011/07-29.

-----. "Barnburner on the Brazos." *Lubbock Avalanche-Journal.* 6 Oct. 2002. http://lubbockonline.com/stories/100602/col_1006020018.shtml.

-----. "Broken Arm Won't Keep Tech's Leach Off Sidelines." *Lubbock Avalanche-Journal.* 9 Oct. 2007. http://lubbockonline.com/stories/100907/col_100907012.shtml.

-----. "Claude Grad, Tech All-American Denton Fox Dies." *Amarillo Globe-News.* 30 April 2013. http://amarillo.com/news/local-news/2013-04-30.

-----. "Coaches Defend Friday Night Hotel Stays as Key in Tech Routine." *Lubbock Avalanche-Journal.* 25 Nov. 2009. http://lubbockonline.com/stories/112509/spo_52860213.shtml.

-----. "Don Williams' 10 Memorable Moments of the Texas Tech-A&M Rivalry." *Red Raiders.com.* 7 Oct. 2011. http://redraiders.com/sports-red-raiders-football/2011-10-07.

-----. "Former Red Raider Took Advantage of Rare Switch." *Lubbock Avalanche-Journal.* 9 Oct. 2005. http://lubbockonline.com/stories/100905/col_100905022.shtml.

-----. "Francis Finds New Challenge on Golf Course." *Lubbock Avalanche-Journal.* 19 Oct. 2002. http://lubbockonline.com/stories/101902/col_1019020036.shtml.

-----. "No. 20 Texas Tech Beats Kansas, 54-16." *Lubbock Avalanche-Journal.* 5 Oct. 2013. http://lubbockonline.com/filed-online/2013-10-05/no-20-texqs-tech-beats-kansas-54-16#.Vd8dXvlViko.

-----. "Playing for Red Raiders All That Richards Ever Wanted." *Lubbock Avalanche-Journal.* 17 Oct. 2014. http://lubbockonline.com/sports-red-raiders-football/2014-10-17/playing-red-raiders-all-richards-ever-wantedE.VeBq-PlViko.

-----. "Raiders Outgun Mississippi." *Lubbock Avalanche-Journal.* 28 Sept. 2003. http://lubbockonline.com/stories/092803/col_092803011.shtml.

-----. "Raiders Strike Late Again." *Lubbock Avalanche-Journal.* 26 Sept. 2004. http://lubbockonline.com/stories/092604/col_092604016.shtml.

-----. "Symons Demonstrates Example of Patience Paying Dividends." *Lubbock Avalanche-Journal.* 1 Nov. 2003. http://lubbockonline.com/stories/110103/col_110103007.shtml.

-----. "Tech Leaves 'Huskers Shell-Shucked." *Lubbock Avalanche-Journal.* 9 Oct. 2005. http://lubbockonline.com/stories/100905/col_100905021.shtml.

-----. "Tech Upsets No. 16 Sun Devils for 37-23 Win in Holiday Bowl." *Lubbock Avalanche-Journal.* 31 Dec. 2013. http://lubbockonline.com/filed-online/2013-12-31/tech-upsets-no-14[*sic*]-sun-devils-37-23-win-holiday-bowl#.Vd9RQ_lViko.

-----. "Tech's Great Late; Aggies Left in Wake." *Lubbock Avalanche-Journal.* 5 Oct. 2003. http://lubbockonline.com/stories/100503/col_100503017.shtml.

-----. "Texas Tech Football Notebook; Players Who Turned Coach Recall '04 Tech-TCU Scene." *Lubbock Avalanche-Journal.* 23 Oct. 2014. http://lubbockonline.com/sports/2014-10-23/texas-tech-football-notebook-players-who-turned-coach-recall-04-tech-tcu-scene#.VeBx0PlViko.

-----. "Texas Tech Names Kingsbury New Head Coach." *Lubbock Avalanche-Journal.* 13 Dec. 2012. http://lubbockonline.com/filed-online/2012-12-12.

-----. "Time to Celebrate: Tech Pulls Off Historic Upset of No. 3 OU." *Lubbock Avalanche-Journal.* 19 Nov. 2007. http://lubbockonline.com/stories/111907/col_111907017.shtml.

-----. "Washington Learned His Lesson Without Kingsbury Yelling." *RedRaiders.com.* 17 Sept. 2013. http://redraiders.com/sports-red-raiders-football/2013-09-17/william/washington-learned-his-lesson.

Wilson, Bernie. "Webb's 4 TD Passes Tie Holiday Bowl Record." *Lubbock Avalanche-Journal.* 31 Dec. 2013. http://lubbockonline.com/filed-online/2013-12-31/webbs-4-td-passes-tie-holiday-bowl-record#.Vd9QGvlViko.

Woodman, Chois. "Luke Adams: Not the Typical Division I Basketball Player." *The Daily Toreador.* 13 Feb. 2012. http://www.dailytoreador.com/sports/article_e35c7e9c-56bb-11d1-b128-001a4bcf6878.html.

Zuvanich, Adam. "Tech Defense Gets Last Word in Overtime." *Lubbock Avalanche-Journal.* 12 Oct 2008. http://lubbockonline.com/stories/101208/spo_343082509.shtml.

NAME INDEX
(LAST NAME, DEVOTION DAY NUMBER)

SCRIPTURES INDEX
(by DEVOTION DAY NUMBER)

RED RAIDERS